Your New Money Mindset lays out a countercultural, proven, and practical approach to managing your relationship with money. Encouraging rather than preachy, Hewitt and Moline make a compelling, biblically grounded case that being wise and generous with your money and time will lead to greater joy, less worry, and a world more the way God intended, and the authors provide actionable steps to get there.

    JONATHAN T. M. RECKFORD, CHIEF EXECUTIVE OFFICER OF HABITAT FOR HUMANITY INTERNATIONAL

Generous giving is something that seems out of reach for the vast majority, and generosity with contentment is only for the very rich, not average, working-class Joes like the rest of us. Enter authors Brad Hewitt and Jim Moline. These gentlemen turn our thinking about contentment, giving, and financial stability on end and ask us to make a radical change, one that begins not with the budget, but with the heart. Whether you're a young family just starting out, or middle aged and trying to navigate college tuition or fast-approaching retirement, they will challenge you to drastically change your attitudes and ideas regarding your finances and giving. They will help you break the persistent desire for more in our consumer-driven society and ask you to reach for something better, something most of us can't see on the financial horizon. That elusive something is peace—the peace that comes with contentment and the decision that we have enough, enough for ourselves and enough to share.

    SHERRY SURRATT, PRESIDENT & CEO OF MOPS, INTERNATIONAL; AUTHOR OF *BRAVE MOM, BEAUTIFUL MESS* AND *JUST LEAD*

In a culture in which financial plans and money tips abound, *Your New Money Mindset* takes us deeper: to the heart. Hewitt and Moline invite families into a soul-healthy approach toward finances, casting a vision extending well beyond bills and 401Ks into the gospel calling of generosity. This fresh perspective beckons us past "how to" into the life-shifting call: "Follow me."

KELLI B. TRUJILLO, EDITOR OF *TODAY'S CHRISTIAN WOMAN*

Imagine sitting down with a Bible and all your finances. Next to you sit two fellow Christians—a psychologist and a financial leader. With warmth, wisdom, and wit, they talk to you about your faith and your money. That important conversation is *Your New Money Mindset*.

LEITH ANDERSON, PRESIDENT OF THE NATIONAL ASSOCIATION OF EVANGELICALS

Brad and Jim demonstrate that while good financial strategies are important, they fail to address the root issue that keeps us in constant angst—our money mindset. How do we achieve a mindset that believes we have more than enough regardless of income and puts us in a position to share it joyfully with others? The authors wisely lead us down the path toward this blessed position. Well written, challenging, and powerful!

PATRICK JOHNSON, CHIEF ARCHITECT OF GENEROUSCHURCH

Brad Hewitt and Jim Moline authentically share their own journey to a healthy relationship with money and challenge us to take the same journey. In *Your New Money Mindset* they connect you with a free online assessment that will help you discover your own money mindset so you can make the necessary adjustments to live the life God dreams for you to live.

DAVE FERGUSON, LEAD PASTOR OF COMMUNITY CHRISTIAN CHURCH, VISIONARY LEADER OF NEWTHING, COAUTHOR OF *FINDING YOUR WAY BACK TO GOD*

Your New Money Mindset is a book that belongs on the shelf of every family who desires to walk in financial freedom. Brad Hewitt and Jim Moline are perfect collaborators, and they have created a resource that will help you have the mind of Christ in the way you view money. The journey you travel with the authors will help you realize your feelings and attitudes about money and how to break free from the debilitating effect of consumerism. Finally, I believe that the transformation that can occur when you experience this New Money Mindset is one that will change the world.

ELLIE KAY, AUTHOR OF *LEAN BODY, FAT WALLET*

Brad Hewitt and Jim Moline do an excellent job of providing eye-opening and practical ways to put your faith into action by nurturing a spirit of generosity, regardless of how much money you may or may not have. I recommend *Your New Money Mindset* as a resource to individuals and congregations, for it contains many nuggets of truth that help you explore your relationship to money and to an incredibly generous God.

M. SARAH BRECKENRIDGE, EXECUTIVE PASTOR OF ST. ANDREW'S LUTHERAN CHURCH, MAHTOMEDI, MN

In *Your New Money Mindset*, Hewitt and Moline persuasively convince us that there is no such thing as "financial security." In this compelling book full of both research and personal narratives, they offer an invitation to go beyond money management to a deeper understanding of the ways our relationship with money has distorted our views of success and our image of "the good life." Mere strategies of self-discipline and delayed gratification are not enough to free us from the bondage of consumerism and the myth we buy into that larger bank accounts will provide the options and affirmation of significance that we are longing for. Investing in a rich relationship with God, living with generosity of time and resources, and practicing the countercultural virtue of contentment are some of the signposts that mark the way on this journey to genuine financial freedom and wisdom.

LAURA ROBINSON HARBERT, PHD, DEAN OF THE CHAPEL AND SPIRITUAL FORMATION, FULLER THEOLOGICAL SEMINARY

Fixing our money problems starts with changing our hearts, and in a world filled with so much noise about finances, Brad and Jim show us how to create real and lasting change. A thought-provoking read, no matter where you are in your financial journey.

RUTH SOUKUP, *NEW YORK TIMES* BESTSELLING AUTHOR OF *LIVING WELL, SPENDING LESS*

It's one thing to say consumerism is like a cancer in our American culture. It certainly is, but many say that. It's another thing to offer a clear, compelling cure for that cancer. That's what Brad and Jim do in *Your New Money Mindset*. The book is filled with assessment tools, stories, Scripture, and personal candor. I want my children and my congregation to read this book.

BILL BOHLINE, LEAD PASTOR OF HOSANNA! LUTHERAN CHURCH; AUTHOR OF *IT'S SUNDAY, BUT MONDAY'S COMIN'*

YOUR NEW MONEY MINDSET

YOUR NEW MONEY MINDSET

CREATE A HEALTHY RELATIONSHIP WITH MONEY

BRAD HEWITT | **JAMES MOLINE**

Tyndale House Publishers, Inc.
Carol Stream, Illinois

Visit Tyndale online at www.tyndale.com.

Learn more about Thrivent Financial at www.thrivent.com.

TYNDALE and Tyndale's quill logo are registered trademarks of Tyndale House Publishers, Inc.

Your New Money Mindset: Create a Healthy Relationship with Money

Designed by Mark Anthony Lane II

Edited by Jane Vogel

ISBN 978-1-4964-0780-1

Printed in the United States of America

21	20	19	18	17	16	15
7	6	5	4	3	2	1

To the founders of Thrivent, who established an effective way for members to help to bear one another's burdens and live generously.

To current members, who model living generously and being wise with money.

To future members, who will join the journey of changing our world for the better.

Contents

Foreword

I REMEMBER IT AS IF IT WERE YESTERDAY. I had started a financial planning practice in 1979 dedicated to helping Christians plan and manage their money well so that they could maximize their giving. It was now just about eighteen months later, and my wife, Judy, and I were taking three very generous couples on a vision trip to Kenya. We had traveled about four hours outside of Nairobi and were visiting with a local pastor. Sitting on a slight hillside looking down at his one-room mud hut as we had tea, I asked him a question that marked me and all the advice that I've given from that time forward. I asked him, "What is the greatest barrier to the spread of the gospel in your part of Africa?" I expected him to say something such as transportation, communication, lack of resources, tribalism, etc. His answer, however, was, "Materialism!" I, probably like you, would never, ever have expected that answer, as

I always associated materialism with America and the accumulation of things. I asked him, "What do you mean?" and he said, "If a man has a mud hut, he wants a stone hut; if he has a thatched roof, he wants a metal roof; if he has one cow, he wants two cows; if he has one acre, he wants two acres." It was then that I realized that materialism is a disease of the heart and has nothing to do with money.

Since that time almost thirty-five years ago, I've had the privilege of helping to build a financial-planning practice that today serves more than seven thousand clients in fifteen locations. I've written several books related to personal biblical financial decision making and been on countless radio shows answering questions. I have learned and observed many things. The most significant thing I have learned is that money decisions are always symptomatic of a belief system. To say it another way, my money mindset drives all my financial decision making, and a mindset is a matter of choice. By definition, it's what I choose to set my mind on. Dallas Willard has said, "The ultimate freedom we have as human beings is the power to select what we will allow our minds to dwell upon."

In our culture today, there are three goals people are most likely to set their minds on—one or all of which drive financial decision making. The three areas people wonder about are, "How much does it take to be successful?," "How much does it take to be significant?," and "How much does it take to be secure?" People easily believe that more money or more "stuff" will answer those questions when, in reality, the answer has very little to do with money and everything to do with a mindset, period.

As I had the privilege of reading the manuscript for this book, I found that the answer to those questions is found in *Your New Money Mindset*. This book is one of the most spiritual that I have ever read, and with good reason. God's Word has more to say about money than any other subject, including prayer, heaven, or hell. Jesus spoke more about money than any other single topic. Jesus, knowing our hearts, told us not to treasure earthly possessions that are doomed to rot and pass away. The answer to "How much is enough?" is always found in my heart, as the African pastor illuminated to me on that day long ago.

The authors of *Your New Money Mindset* provide a very practical tool to help me assess my money mindset. I need to know where I am before I can begin to deal with getting to where I really want to go. In chapter 11, Brad and Jim disclose where they want to go and what they care about in their lives: "having authentic faith, strengthening Christian communities where we live, being wise with our money and generous with our lives. We know these changes happen only by God's grace and power."

I would encourage you to reflect on this first and see their hearts before you read their advice. They know and share that money is one of the tools that God has given you to help you get to where he wants you to go. He has designed you uniquely, gifted you uniquely, and called you uniquely. He has given you money and wisdom to help along the way. My experience is that when we have an eternal perspective (mindset), follow God's principles of money management, and seek his wisdom, the end result includes three key factors. We experience a life of *contentment*, because everything is in its proper perspective. We act with *confidence*, because God's principles will never change—they're always relevant, and they're always right. Finally, we experience outstanding *communication* with those that we need to communicate with, most likely our spouses, because we are seeking God's goals and not ours.

This is a great book, and I have been privileged to review it and write this foreword. I am praying that this book will impact families, churches, and communities with the good news of the Kingdom of God.

Ron Blue
Founding Director, Kingdom Advisors

CHAPTER 1

OUR MONEY PROBLEM

RYAN WAS NEVER A FAN OF SCHOOL, and after a couple of years of college he hit the job market just as the Internet was becoming an essential part of everyday life. He has an eye for web design and a knack for coding, and he worked for other people long enough to save up cash and strike out on his own. In good years, his new business has thrived. In several not-so-good years, Ryan is proud to say he has survived.

Alycia fell in love with this creative, driven entrepreneur. The couple met as twenty-three-year-olds playing in a church softball league. Alycia and Ryan dreamed of a growing business with more impact and an increasing bottom line. They envisioned a life more affluent than either of them had enjoyed while growing up. After the couple married, Alycia continued her career in human relations. When she gave birth to a daughter followed by a son a year later, she chose to work part time, and she continues to find steady employment a decade and a half later. Both Ryan and Alycia feel they have accomplished much but long for more. They want a bigger house in a more prestigious neighborhood, for example, but they will stay in place as long as they owe more on their mortgage than their house is worth.

Ryan has felt increasing business pressure for the past several years. In fact, his company would shrink if he didn't put in longer days than ever. He feels as if he is barely holding his own as he competes with innumerable kids half his age who are promoting themselves as experts in all things digital. Inexpensive do-it-yourself design platforms mean Ryan's expertise isn't valued even when it is badly needed.

Business has gone flat just at the time family expenses are exploding. With a daughter in her junior year of high school and a son a year behind, spending feels out of control. Ryan used to think it was ridiculous when little Bekka wanted a hundred-dollar doll and a tubful of accessories. Now the latest cell phone and a closetful of clothes are just the start. His son once played endlessly with a glove and ball. Last week

Daniel came home and announced he needed hundreds of dollars of lacrosse equipment the next day.

Although the couple struggles to make vehicle payments, they keep rolling over leases on new models. Ryan once vowed his family would never own more than two cars, but when Bekka earned her driver's license, he realized an extra car would make it easier for her to get to club-soccer activities. Soon a third vehicle appeared in the driveway, and lately Ryan has wondered about getting a fourth one. Not that there's anywhere to park it. The space is already occupied by an SUV and trailer for hauling Daniel's motocross bike and a spare to races.

Even though the college clock is ticking down for their children, Ryan and Alycia block that from their minds. Ryan assures Alycia that if he just has a consistent stream of business, he can write checks to cover tuition. They need to convince Bekka and Daniel to enroll in public universities close to home, but both kids have other ideas. The children might need sizable loans to cover their schooling, but these days, who doesn't?

Ryan sees himself as an astute, self-made man. Thanks to his hard work and Alycia's contributions, they have always lived well. They look like they make a lot more money than they do. Ryan is living the dream of being his own boss. Alycia always has a confident, put-together look, and the couple is popular with other parents at school and church. Those relationships create demands to spend money on going out, weekend getaways, and even group vacations, but Ryan and Alycia feel like those outings are investments in their family.

Lately Ryan rolls out of bed feeling that every day is make or break. Landing the next client will secure him weeks or months of work, and until the next shortfall, he feels pretty good. When he has hit lean stretches, extended family have helped with loans. Ryan dreads the day someone discovers he often borrows from one family member to pay off another. Not long ago Alycia went behind his back to get money from her parents and from a sibling who has less but still feels sorry for her. Although they never speak about it, Ryan and Alycia both wonder when the life they work so hard to maintain will all fall apart.

Our Money Relationship
It's tough to blame Ryan and Alycia for wanting a better life. They're good people. Hard workers. A husband and wife in love. Parents who want the best for their kids. They're committed to God. If you were looking for someone to hang out with, they would probably be high on your list.

At the same time that we empathize with Ryan and Alycia's desire to have a nice life, we can't help but notice their unhealthy relationship with money. Our *money relationship* is our everyday attitudes and actions toward money—how we think and feel about money, and how we use or misuse it. Like any relationship, it can be good or bad, healthy or unhealthy, on the upswing or on life support.

Our money relationship *is our everyday attitudes and actions toward money.*

When Ryan and Alycia think about money, they are detached from reality. They keep spending more and more even as they get closer and closer to the edge of a cliff. They live each day worrying they will get caught. Their affluence is more or less a costume and their self-reliance a mask. Deep inside they experience self-doubt. They fear their way of life will come crashing down, and their most basic needs will go unmet.

Unfortunately, almost everywhere we turn, we observe unhealthy dynamics around money. We notice it not just in grown-ups struggling to keep up in a culture of discontent. We also observe it in young people trying hard to make their way in the world. And to be honest, we see the battle raging within ourselves.

Money Madness

As authors we want to tell you something that might shock you: we don't claim to have this money problem all figured out. We struggle against the same impulses everyone does, and we are comfortable admitting it. Why? Because it's true. Consumerism is the air we all breathe. It fills our lungs and pumps through every part of our being. If you don't realize we fight the same battles you do, you could easily conclude we don't have anything to offer you regarding your own relationship with money.

We do bring backgrounds that help us understand this money problem so we can move ourselves and others toward a new solution. We come from different perspectives. Brad is the CEO of Thrivent Financial, a Fortuné 500 company that is also a membership organization of Christians. The organization is more than a hundred years old and serves over two million members. Jim is a PhD licensed psychologist with a graduate degree in theology. A former university professor and clinical therapist, Jim now leads people to excellence in the world of work. We are both immersed in business, in non-profit causes near and far, and in the daily life of local church congregations.

The quick handle on us is that Brad knows math and money. Jim understands beliefs and behavior. We also both know Jesus. We are enthusiastic in our commitment to live as his followers, and we believe our relationship with him integrates with every part of life. Including money.

Jim has two daughters on the threshold of adulthood. Mira is a recent university graduate, and Asha is just beginning college. Both are highly responsible with their money. Even so, some days Jim hears them wonder aloud, "How can I pursue a profession I love and still earn an adequate living after paying off my school loans?" He senses some fear that they won't earn enough money to buy a home or even a dependable car. Underneath it all, he wonders if his daughters are really saying, "I don't feel very hopeful about my financial future" or "I'm never going to be happy."

Our culture makes it nearly impossible for any of us to be content. There is always a new iPhone or iPad or iSomething coming out. When everyone else is sprinting full-out in a race to have more, it's tough to stand on the sidelines. We frequently hear stories about emerging young adults who, soon after they acquire a credit card, owe far more within a month than they have means to pay back. If children grow up accustomed to parents paying for everything from a Wii to their wardrobe, computers to cars, they seek to extend that lifestyle by almost any means necessary.

We have always known that young people who don't pursue training or education beyond high school are often doomed to scuffling through life in low-paying jobs. Yet many who get the step-up that more schooling affords remain at risk of a lifetime of falling behind. Ask around among young adults, and many talk freely about taking on enormous student debt. They start life so far behind that they will catch up only with great effort.

Without adequate savings from family or money they accumulate on their own, most students take loans to make it to graduation. Debt that can be repaid without causing a painful burden can open doors to the right job and a fulfilling adulthood. But many students pile up debt to enter jobs that don't pay enough to ever dig out. Students dream of helping the world through teaching. Or church work. Or they want to make a statement through music or fill the world with beautiful art. But having $80,000 in loans darkens those aspirations. These young people carry the incredible burden of not being free to live out their calling. Others use their loans to fund nonessentials. Many wind up with huge debt and no degree.

Brad serves on the board of an urban Christian university in Minnesota. The board has worked aggressively to cut tuition and make it more affordable. Why? They want the school to remain a viable option for students from all economic backgrounds. They also feel a moral obligation to the sons and daughters who attend the school. Until the board intervened, some students were living in their cars—and anecdotal evidence suggests that a significant percentage of students attending public and for-profit colleges do the same.

Student finances are a crisis in our country. How does all of this madness happen? It is the constant press of consumer culture that pushes young people to do things that just don't add up.

Pictures That Say It All

Thrivent Financial, where Brad is CEO, started an enterprise—**brightpeak**—to reach young families. Part of brightpeak's mission is to offer free or low-cost financial education to young adults. Through brightpeak research to develop their service offerings, they asked participants to draw pictures of their relationships with money and to talk about the pictures. What they said—well, a few pictures are worth millions of words.

I'm in the middle of a spiderweb, being pulled out from all directions. I feel helpless and alone, stuck, stretched, scared. Here comes the financial future spider ready to swallow me up. He's overwhelming and dominating. There's not enough money for what I need now and the future. It feels out of reach. My finances are my day-to-day driving force, the basis of every decision I make, and that's overwhelming.

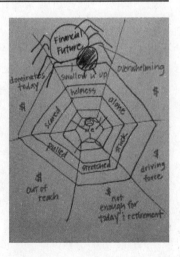

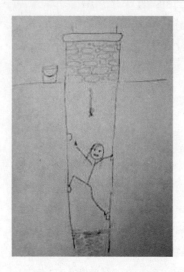

I often feel like I'm climbing out of a well. I'm still toward the bottom, I have different handholds. Climbing up is more difficult because it gets wider—there are fewer handholds to get myself out.

I'm driving a train, singing *la la la*. I don't realize that I'm going to fall off the tracks onto jagged rocks.

My future is in question. A scale: on the left side is the present, on the right side is the future. We're so bogged down by things we need to pay for in the present, we're finally getting to the point where we're at our peak, making enough to enjoy life, but there are all these things we have to pay for. You end up living paycheck to paycheck, even if you don't want to. The unexpected is included in there, upkeep, what happens if the dog gets sick, if the furnace goes out. Things that keep bogging you down and keeping the balance way off. We haven't been able to equal it, and the future is a big question mark.

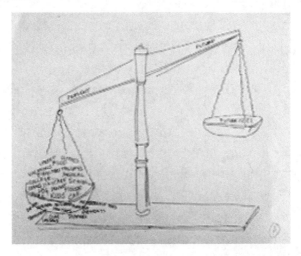

Our Money Problem

We could each draw our own pictures of our money relationship—a depiction of our attitudes and actions about money. The discussion guide at the back of this book will invite you to do that. But this sample of participants' pictures and their brief descriptions captures the thoughts and feelings of many. Those attitudes are pervasive whether you're a single mom raising three kids and barely getting by or a two-income family that pulls in $200,000 a year yet feels detached from each other and your community. These dynamics transcend economic and educational categories. Many of us carry a burden of money unease, tension, or panic. Many feel a distinct need to keep up appearances. Many feel an urgent desire for more and bigger and better. And the research we will examine shows we feel the press of consumerism no matter how much or how little we have.

Consumerism is our desire to acquire more for ourselves when we already have enough. It's our obsession with money and all it can buy. While consumerism is driven by external culture pressures— such as the barrage of advertisements we see each day or the comparisons we make against our peers— it takes root and grows inside human hearts.

There are many concrete measures of consumerism's grip on us. We could add up personal credit-card debt and car loans and other consumer expenditures, then compare that total with our annual income. We might immediately discover how badly overextended we are. We could journal about the times and places we spend money we don't have. Or we could look deeper and assess the money attitudes that drive us. We think that last approach is most revealing. As we will see throughout this book, our thoughts and feelings about money are where helpful or harmful behaviors start.

Most people have never examined a belief held at the deepest part of their hearts and minds. As consumers, we think that the greatest good we can accomplish is to spend more. We anxiously watch the growth or contraction of our economy and count it a civic duty to boost the gross domestic product (GDP). And we are driven to obtain more and bigger and better for ourselves. Researcher Jon Alexander points out that this consumer drive—as measured by short-term, personal, material standards—breeds a self-interest that spreads to every area of life. Consumerism shapes our habits not just at the mall or the car lot but in our homes, our political maneuverings, our investing, and beyond.[1] At its worst, consumerism feeds an unrestrained selfishness throughout life.

> Consumerism *is our desire to acquire more for ourselves when we already have enough.*

As Christian leaders, we see this trend in the church. People show up less as worshipers or community members than as consumers. As soon as an engaging preacher leaves or a great musician moves on, the church down the road suddenly looks a lot better. That's a consumer mindset, and it makes it difficult to grow communities of believers fully committed to God, to each other, and to their world.

You can't live in the modern world and not be affected by consumerism. Without intervention, those longings to acquire more just never go away. We think, *If I could just buy that new thing, I would be content. If I could just have that next job, I would finally be successful. If I just had a big stock port-folio, I would be secure. If I just had my retirement all figured out, I wouldn't have to rely on anyone else.* Most of all, we live with a persistent misbelief that if we just had a little more, we would be happy forever.

We live with a persistent misbelief that if we just had a little more, we would be happy forever.

But this is an unending cycle. It goes round and round. That's the consumer lie. That's our money problem.

Welcome to the Struggle

You might be a person active in your faith who already thinks faith and finances go together. Or you might be unsure about any part of that equation—your basic beliefs, the right way to relate to money, or the compatibility of God and money. Wherever you are right now, we want to invite you to come with us on a journey where we discover how one of life's most practical issues is impacted by a new mindset only the gospel can bring. We will reexamine some fundamental assumptions, see how Jesus turns portions of our thinking upside down, and explore how to put potent new ideas into practice. If you are looking for transformation at points of your life that really matter, you will find it here.

There are three reasons we think this journey is incredibly important to all of us.

First, *Jesus makes money a crucial topic*. It's impossible to miss in Scripture how often he talks about our unhealthy relationship with money and how easily we make money an idol that usurps the place of more important things. Jesus aims to lead us to life, and we can think of nothing better than that.

Second, *this journey will change you*. However you would describe your feelings about money—unease, tension, bondage, discouragement, dissatisfaction, even boredom—we want to help you break free from the debilitating effects of consumerism. No matter where you are on the socioeconomic ladder, we will show you how to thrive personally, as a family unit, and as an active part of a community.

Third, *the transformation you experience will change the world*. We believe that if people—especially Christians—could have a healthier relationship with money, it would change the world. We envision a world of human flourishing where both a financial sense of well-being and a joyful generosity prevail. We believe change can happen better, faster, and further than any of us thinks possible. We truly believe that people can be free from the slavery of a consumer culture by having a right relationship with money as taught by Jesus and other voices of Scripture, and as a result they will live openheartedly with their time, energy, and money.

In our day-to-day lives we often fail to see wisdom because authentic understanding doesn't tend to be showy. People who have grown a healthy relationship with money have a contentment and quietness that is attractive but not flashy. Their hearts and minds are at rest. They travel at a sustainable and appealing pace. We believe this way of life is possible for anyone, regardless of financial circumstance, because living freely doesn't depend on how much money you have or don't have. Research and real-life examples prove that.

Imagine a life where you control your money instead of your money controlling you. If you find yourself wrestling with credit-card debt you can't pay off, or a car you can't afford, or a house worth less than you owe on it, keep reading. If you long to feel more satisfied at the end of each day because you have given yourself to something more than the fleeting gratification of another online purchase, this book is for you. If you want to help family and friends break free from debt and consumerism, we believe we have insights from Scripture that will help. This is a book for people who want the life-giving, grace-filled, abundant life of Scripture.

Join Us on the Journey

This is the journey we are on. Do you want to come with us? We hope so. We think you need to. Research says that the two biggest struggles reported by multi-multi-millionaires are isolation and anxiety about their kids—that their children will screw up the money they have.[2] If people aren't happy with millions and millions of dollars, tens of millions of dollars, hundreds of millions of dollars, this money problem affects everyone. We're pretty sure it touches you. And Jesus offers hope.

It used to be that four subjects were taboo to discuss around the dining room table—sex, politics, religion, and money. Today the only topic you can't mention is money. Conversation about money is considered impolite. Everyone wants to bolt for the door when the pastor preaches on finances, knowing that a guilt-inducing pitch for more giving probably comes next. Can you imagine bringing up money at a holiday gathering with your in-laws? And yet how we relate to money drives many of our behaviors and dictates much of the good and bad of our lives.

We want to invite you into an honest dialogue with us—and with yourself. We also think it would be helpful for you to initiate a conversation with people in your immediate world. We don't think you should talk about how much money you make or even how many dollars are enough to have the life you dream of. There are deeper issues to explore. Chances are, whatever goes on inside you about money is a lot like what churns inside the person next to you.

Taking this journey with others makes it immensely more enjoyable and effective. Both of us have financial guides who are also Christian who help our families think hard about money and make wise choices. We have peers and mentors who let us air both our frustrations and our breakthroughs. Likewise, we encourage you to invite a companion or two along for this trip. You can read this book in the context of a small group of friends or maybe even get a whole community talking. We have included discussion questions in an appendix to guide you.

So risk being a little impolite. Start a conversation. When you break your silence about money, you begin to loosen its grip.

Your Next Step

So something needs to change—but where do you start? How do you remake a bad relationship with money? Or how do you take a good relationship with money to even greater levels of health? What is the first step on this journey?

Countless books and other resources will give you the nuts and bolts of making smarter financial decisions. Much of the advice you will find is helpful. But when it comes to your real money problem, we want to offer you a radically different solution. Before you can remake your habits, you need to remake your heart.

Before you can remake your habits, you need to remake your heart.

You have probably tried to "do better with money" through brute force, bringing willpower to bear on what you identify as problem areas. But a better relationship with money begins with the heart. Altering how you think and feel is the only realistic way to bring about a lasting difference in how you act.

We think that our calling attention to this primary issue is unique among advice you will hear about dealing with money. The truths we will share have been effective in helping ourselves and many others. We have told you a bit about the problem. In chapter 2 we will let you in on more of the solution. And in chapter 3 we will introduce an exciting assessment to help you look at your relationship with money and begin to determine your own next steps to a new money mindset.

CHAPTER 2

A NEW MONEY MINDSET

WE WERE LUNCHING on a sunny riverfront patio, watching the Mississippi push past northeast Minneapolis. In a place that serves up tater tots, burgers, and pizza, the South Pacific décor of Psycho Suzi's is both jarring and amusing. It's a tiki-themed mashup the owners dub "faux paradise."

As we ate, we discussed our usual topics. Family. Work. Life. God. Brad talked about plans to lead his organization through significant change. On a more personal note, his daughter had just graduated from college and was preparing to fly away for two years as a Peace Corps volunteer. Jim was busy helping his own daughter pick a school for her undergraduate studies. Between the two of us, we offered up plenty of concrete items for prayer. Much of our conversational ground that day was well traveled, but we also talked at length about a bigger topic we had circled for years.

The idea that dominated our conversation was how consumerism drives a tragically large percentage of people to money problems much like those eating away at Ryan and Alycia, the couple we introduced in chapter 1. Some of these people bring home modest or average incomes, but others are high earners. The details of each story differ, but all reveal an unhealthy money relationship that creates a sense of unease, tension, or panic. Even when these people have enough, they feel an urgent desire for more and bigger and better. Not a few have built their own version of "faux paradise" only to watch it blow away in the storms of life.

The consequences of this unhealthy relationship with money are not only practical and financial but also spiritual, emotional, and relational. Money struggles can create animosity toward God and raise questions about his care. They sap our emotional well-being. And they can devastate our interactions with people—spouses, immediate and extended family, friends, coworkers, and communities. Personal observations, countless one-on-one and group conversations, and a variety of research provide abundant evidence for these conclusions.

While this weary mass of people composes a large majority of modern society, we have also met a distinctly different set of individuals far more at peace with money. Some are high earners, but many others bring home average or even modest incomes. What do they have in common? They have all undergone a transformation in how they think about money and material things, and as a result they feel free from the drive to acquire more and more for themselves. They are more likely to feel satisfied with what they already have, and their days are not preoccupied with money and all it can buy.

The more readily we share our time, energy, and money, the more joy we discover in life.

These friends and neighbors and strangers live in the same world we do. So they aren't exempt from the press of consumer culture—constant marketing messages or the temptation to compare themselves to peers—but their hearts overflow with more important things. They have formed healthy money relationships. They have a new money mindset. And they have discovered a secret we want to let you in on: the more readily we share our time, energy, and money, the more joy we discover in life.

Principles into Practice

Many of us know enough sound money-management tips to tell friends like Ryan and Alycia how to put their finances in order. Ryan needs a revamped, realistic business plan. Alycia could pick up more hours at work, and the kids might find part-time jobs. The family must establish a spending plan and live within their means. They should take action to eliminate debt. They must reevaluate their wants and needs, and they need to learn to delay gratification for the sake of their long-term financial well-being. If Ryan and Alycia obtain and act on solid professional counsel, so we might say, they will be well on their way to improving their credit, building wealth, retiring when they choose, and blessing their children with an inheritance. It's as easy as . . .

If only it were that easy. Those are all wise money strategies, and there are many more we could list. But we can know the rules and not get the desired results. Why? While it's easy to dispense advice, we all know that putting wisdom into practice is another matter. Especially for the long haul. Today you might get a good start. Tomorrow will bring new trials and temptations. After days, weeks, or longer, you could find yourself back where you started or worse.

We honestly believe good money strategies—by themselves—cannot end the cycle of money problems once and for all. If we want the power to make and live out wise money choices, we start with the heart. Without changing our inner attitudes toward money, it's unlikely we will succeed in remaking our outward behaviors. We might even unintentionally encourage and accelerate our consumer ambitions. To the extent we do succeed, we will feel the strain that comes from forcing ourselves forward through brute willpower.

As soon as we start talking in terms of better money habits we "must" and "should" implement, we need to tap a more powerful solution. If we want to truly break free from the consumerism that drives us, we must develop a new money mindset.

Money Mindsets

Using research conducted by Thrivent Financial,[1] we have identified five distinct attitudes people hold toward money—five ways of relating to all that they have and own. These "money mindsets" describe how people think and feel about their financial well-being—or lack of it. Since each category begins with the letter S, we call these the "5Ss." But before we tell you about each S, you first must hear a truth: the health of your relationship with money is not determined by how much money you have or don't have.

Most people believe that the more money they earn or otherwise possess, the healthier their relationship with money will be. That point might seem self-evident, but it's an illusion. This myth will become clearer as we define the 5S categories, and we will explore its deceptiveness in all the pages that follow. Put succinctly, you can have a high income yet struggle. Or you can have a modest income yet thrive.

The health of your relationship with money is not determined by how much money you have or don't have.

As we explain the 5S categories, you will notice a gradually improving relationship with money. But we believe that only one attitude delivers the deep peace and freedom we desire. We believe that only what we call the "surplus" mindset is healthy through and through.

Money Attitudes among Christians in the United States

It's amazing. In the richest country in the world,

- Nearly 50 percent of Christians feel financially insecure.
- More than 85 percent of Christians feel they do not have enough to share generously.

Again, our relationship with money is not *determined* by how much money we have or don't have. While it can *affect* our money mindset, the amount is not as significant as what we do with what we have.[2]

THE 5S ATTITUDES TOWARD MONEY

Relationship with Money	*Unhealthy*	**Surviving:** *Feeling drained, trapped, with little sense of hope* People who are *surviving* worry about meeting the basic needs of life, and every bit of what they earn goes to daily survival. Most in this group require financial assistance or a helping hand to get by. This group accounts for 6 percent of Christians in the United States.
		Struggling: *Feeling strapped in the present and anxious about the future* Money causes much of the stress felt by those who are *struggling*. As financial pressures build, relationships with families, friends, and communities often begin to crack. Strugglers live paycheck to paycheck—or worse, slowly dig themselves deeper into debt. This group accounts for 11 percent of US Christians. Until recently it was the fastest-growing segment.
		Stable: *Feeling okay, experiencing relative calm but hoping for more* The stress level of the *stable* might be a bit lower, but they don't yet feel secure. They don't plan much for the future and likely aren't as generous as they want to be. They describe themselves as "just making ends meet," and while this group doesn't live paycheck to paycheck, they are one disaster away from real hardship. This group accounts for 32 percent of US Christians.
		Secure: *Feeling mostly confident* Those in the group we call *secure* feel they have enough for themselves but probably not enough extra to share generously. As their income grows so do lifestyle expenses, so they perpetually have "just enough," with only a little extra. Although having a financial strategy might increase their sense of security, these people can be as enslaved to saving as strugglers are to debt. This group encompasses 38 percent of US Christians.
	Healthy	**Surplus:** *Feeling grateful and ready to share* Members of the *surplus* group believe they have more than enough. They don't constantly long for more. They display a high level of contentment even if their lifestyle is average—or below. Their purchases match their needs, not their income. And because they feel grateful, they are ready to share. Most joyfully give away more than 10 percent of their gross income. Only 13 percent of US Christians feel they live in surplus.

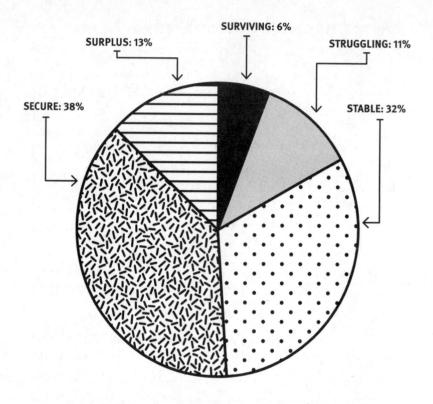

Many people with modest incomes show the peace and generosity of living in a surplus mindset. Many others who have accumulated outward wealth can be described only as struggling. Even earners at the highest levels of income often have profound concerns about their financial security. They are not automatically happier than those with less.

How can this be? It turns out that making more money doesn't equate to feeling financially secure or having an impulse to share. Ratcheting up income doesn't bestow the peace and freedom experienced by those who have decided they have enough to share, even if "enough" doesn't include trappings of the so-called good life. "Enough" might not look like much to anyone else, but people with a surplus mindset experience an amazing state of contentment.

A "surplus" mindset means deciding we have enough for ourselves and enough to share.

Remember: a surplus mindset isn't about how much we have. It's a conscious choice to think and act differently about everything we own or might wish we did. A surplus mindset means deciding we have enough for ourselves and enough to share.

The surplus mindset is where we all want to live. It's the "new money mindset" we aim to grow into, and one of our goals in this book is to help you take your own next steps toward that way of thinking and living. No matter where you are right now, you can begin to move forward. But if that healthy money mindset is where we want to go, how do we get there?

Growing a New Money Mindset

We wish we could tell you that we have perfectly mastered our relationship with money. We would love to say we never slip from contentment to restlessness. But we want to be honest with you. We notice that we can migrate between healthy and unhealthy attitudes from month to month, day to day, or even moment to moment.

I (Brad) met my wife at a ski hill. Our children learned to ski early, squealing with glee as they whooshed downhill between our legs. Nowadays our kids regularly beat their parents to the bottom, but we all still cherish time on the snow as some of our best family moments.

Years ago we purchased a fractional ownership in a Colorado townhouse, which grants us two weeks of winter access. All year long I look forward to basking in the Rocky Mountain grandeur. I count on it to sweep me into God's presence and renew an appreciation of all his good gifts. But even as those wonders fill me, they can also put my heart into a frenzy faster than I like to admit. One minute I'm thanking God for his blessings. The next I'm gawking at a new row of bigger and better vacation homes and thinking, *I want one.* To be clear, I don't need one. Coming back to the familiar townhouse always feels like a lavish blessing. By any measure we already have more than enough. Nevertheless, my gratitude can quickly be displaced by a longing for more.

At the moment those misguided desires well up inside me, I face a choice. I can continue to stare at the thing I want. I can obsess over it all the way home. I can calculate what a fancy new place costs. I can loudly convince myself and my family that I need it. Or I can act to break that cycle.

We break our persistent desire for more when we choose to live generously. I'm not talking about an occasional act of benevolence. The solution to my yearning for a bigger and better place isn't to ski to the bottom of the hill and write a one-time check to a worthy cause. The long-term fix is cultivating a day-by-day pattern of openhearted giving. It's pursuing a way of life that puts a happy generosity first.

We break our persistent desire for more when we choose to live generously.

God invites all of us to live in a new money mindset, to recognize that we have enough for ourselves and enough to share. His call is not to get in line for more money or better stuff but to think as he does and to use money and possessions in ways that reach far beyond ourselves. But that new mindset doesn't come automatically.

As the chart on page 28 shows, only 13 percent of US Christians exhibit behaviors that demonstrate contentment in both attitudes and actions. Let's face it. Our normal human pattern is to wait to give until we think we have ample money. Only when we're sure we have excess beyond our own needs and wants do we consider acting generously toward others.

We need to turn our thinking on end. Rather than

letting the amount of money we have determine our ability to be generous, we want to start with generosity. When we choose to give first, we begin to grow a healthier relationship with money.

This isn't a gimmick. When you give, you won't suddenly have more money, even if some preachers promise you an instant and abundant return on your act of giving. But as your mindset shifts, you will gain a clearer sense of your priorities in managing what you already have. And if you have difficult financial changes to make, you will take those steps feeling greater freedom and power. The act of being gracious to others begins an inward and outward transformation.

When we choose to give first, we begin to grow a healthier relationship with money.

By the way, generosity isn't just about money. It's also about sharing your whole self—time, energy, wisdom, talents, attention, compassion, empathy, and more. It's doing simple acts that make a difference for a neighbor nearby or on the other side of the world. You might feel like you don't have money to give. That's okay. Generosity is about far more than cash. It's a fundamental change from keeping everything for ourselves to finding ways to bless others.

Jesus once climbed a hillside to teach a crowd clamoring around him. He had a habit of talking about the real stuff of life, and it didn't take long for

Jesus to get around to money and possessions. He recognized that this crowd had little more than the clothes on their backs and the walking sticks in their hands. Hardly any of his listeners had storehouses filled with months of provisions. Few of them would ever be financially well off. Nevertheless, Jesus challenged them to pray only for daily bread and not to get worked up about possessions. He said, "Don't hoard treasure down here where it gets eaten by moths and corroded by rust or—worse!—stolen by burglars. Stockpile treasure in heaven, where it's safe from moth and rust and burglars. It's obvious, isn't it? The place where your treasure is, is the place you will most want to be, and end up being" (Matthew 6:19-21, MSG).

Jesus assured his listeners that they could live freely because God knew their needs and would meet those needs. *The Message* paraphrase says well what Jesus aimed to accomplish: "What I'm trying to do here is to get you to relax, to not be so preoccupied with *getting*, so you can respond to God's *giving*" (Matthew 6:31).

Grounded in Grace
God's gifts to us are where our generosity starts. Even in the midst of enormous struggles, we can still step out in sharing, knowing that God promises to care

for our real needs. Whenever generosity feels like an impossibility, we can revisit what God has done for us.

We live generously toward others when we are grounded in God's grace toward us, because we can't manufacture joyful generosity on our own. Our Creator and Redeemer is the ultimate source. Without grasping how generous God has been with us, any steps we take toward openheartedness will be an onerous duty.

We live generously toward others when we are grounded in God's grace toward us.

A famous interaction between Jesus and a woman at a well gives a good view of God's generosity. It was a hot summer day when the woman realized she was thirsty. She must have stared out the window of her home at the village's parched ground, wondering if it was safe to go outside. She had already been married five times and was living with yet another man, and she did all she could to avoid the scorn of her neighbors. The sun was sweltering, but in the noontime heat she was unlikely to run into anyone. She stepped outside, picked up a clay jar, and headed for the town well.

The woman was surprised to see a stranger sitting at the well's edge, even more so when he asked her for a drink. Taken aback, she asked why he would speak to her when their tribes were enemies. He said, "If you knew the generosity of God and who I am, you would be asking *me* for a drink, and I would give you fresh, living water" (John 4:10, MSG).

She was confused. The man repeated the promise of living water, prompting the woman to ask for this water. That's when Jesus revealed all he knew about her life, and despite her being an ethnic enemy and regardless of her gritty life, he offered her a gift—a new path, the way to a well of living water that never runs dry, the gift of himself. She was so excited that she ran through the village telling people they had to come hear this rabbi.

Jesus' coming into our world is an act of God's generosity. But it's far from the only way God extends his gracious care. The generosity shown in Christ comes to us in many ways right here and now:

Creation: God's grace is evident everywhere. Marvelous oceans enwrap our world, holding riches that inspire wonder. Birds of limitless color and song flash through the air. Trees and plants and flowers beautify our planet. Animals of every shape and size dot the land and cause us to pause at their majesty. And humans complete the story. Blended in color, custom, history, and religion, we seven billion people share the same genetic codes but weave a tapestry of infinite distinction. Ours is a world graciously and generously supplied by God.

Community: God gives us family—biological and adopted—along with friends, neighbors, churches, and other communities where we love and support one another and enjoy God's gifts. God also extends grace to us by choosing to be with us as we gather. Where two or three join in his name, Jesus says, he will be with us (see Matthew 18:20).

Purpose: God offers us a life with meaning—not a self-centered sense of satisfaction but an impactful service for the good of others. Some of the most appealing characters in the Bible were women and men who served (Ruth, Rahab, Naomi, Daniel, Joseph, Philemon, and many others). We believe that once we discover our calling, we can be energized to give of ourselves in ways that deepen our sense that we have made a difference.

Forgiveness: Human brokenness taints all of God's gifts. The creation is spoiled by greed. Communities are fractured by selfishness. Many individuals live aimless lives. Despite God's generosity, we turn our backs on him. What is his response to our pride, selfishness, and ungratefulness? Here's how the apostle Paul put it: "God demonstrates his own love for us in this: While we were still sinners, Christ died for us" (Romans 5:8). And in the Gospel of John we read this: "God so loved the world that he gave his one and only Son, that whoever believes in him shall not perish but have eternal life" (John 3:16).

God's forgiveness extends to every part of life, including money mistakes and sins. If you carry a weight of unwise choices or even wrongdoing, admit what you have done wrong to God and to the people directly involved, repair what you can as best you can, and move forward with God's fresh start.

This is the ultimate expression of God's generosity, the forgiveness he offers through Christ's death on the cross. By coming to earth and dying in our place, Jesus made clear God's method, message, and means. It's all about sacrificial love. From God to us, *This new money mindset breathes life into our soul.* and from us to others. "We love," says the writer of 1 John, "because God first loved us" (4:19, NCV).

Greater Joy

Jesus longs for us to experience the delight that comes from responding generously to God's giving. As the ancient words of Psalm 4:7 tell us, "You have given me greater joy than those who have abundant harvests of grain and new wine" (NLT).

This new money mindset breathes life into

our soul: "Get wisdom—it's worth more than money; choose insight over income every time" (Proverbs 16:16, MSG). It alters how we get along with others: "The world of the generous gets larger and larger; the world of the stingy gets smaller and smaller" (Proverbs 11:24, MSG). It releases us into a deeper relationship with God: "No one can serve two masters. For you will hate one and love the other; you will be devoted to one and despise the other. You cannot serve both God and money" (Matthew 6:24).

Starting with generosity—no matter the size of our bank account—might sound as offbeat as cheese curds in a palm-thatched eatery on the banks of the northern Mississippi. Yet sharing our time, energy, and money—all that we are—is how we break free from the crowd and become those rare people at peace with money. What matters isn't whether our income is large or small but that we are transformed in how we think about material things, becoming less preoccupied with money and more satisfied with what we have. This transformation empowers us to be done with the consumer mentality that says we always need more when we already have enough. As adopted children of our generous God, we indeed already have more than we need.

This new way of thinking doesn't come naturally to any of us. The new money mindset defies the consumerism that infects our culture and sickens our hearts. And to let this new attitude truly take hold of us, we need to be convinced that it works in real life. For the remainder of this book, we will examine our most common thoughts and actions around money, challenging inadequate ideas and building a better outlook. To move us on our way, chapter 3 will introduce you to an exciting assessment to help you uncover specific attitudes that help or hinder you.

CHAPTER 3

READY

AT THE END OF MY FIRST EXPERIENCE living away at college, I (Brad) was moving out of my dorm room and heading home for the summer. My roommate and I decided to split our earthly possessions, sorting out exactly what belonged to whom. You can imagine the contents of our shared room. We were a couple of guys scraping through school, and what we owned was next to worthless. Most of our things were worn out when we got them, and we further used and abused them. Almost all of the possessions Kurt and I hovered over belonged in a Dumpster.

Still I dug in. I resolved that I had to have our

stained, threadbare couch and a ratty old carpet remnant. I negotiated hard for those treasures. And I won. I was gloating over my prizes when Kurt took the opportunity to call me out. He told me I was greedy and selfish.

Coming from a gracious and generous guy who remains one of my best friends, his words hit hard. They triggered a long process of examining my attitude toward money and possessions. Would I spend my life collecting things for myself—for my own pleasure and satisfaction—or would I share what I had for the benefit of others?

Struggling Forward

Most of us need prompting to think through our relationship with money—our everyday attitudes and actions toward it and all that it can buy. We don't naturally pause and evaluate our money mindset— particularly how our thoughts and feelings impact our ability to be generous with all that we have and are. And it's challenging for us to consider the idea of "giving first" with the goal of growing a healthier relationship with money—especially when we are confronted by concrete struggles:

- "My emergency savings are at zero."
- "College tuition bills for my kids are right around the corner."

- "I finally got a job that pays well, I'm working nonstop, and I need to reward myself."
- "My house is significantly underwater."
- "I hate when my family spends my hard-earned money, even on things we need."
- "Everyone I know has more money than I do—it's their turn to be generous."
- "I'm scared about my lack of retirement savings."
- "I teeter on the edge of bankruptcy."
- "I don't know how long I will be healthy enough to work."

We might assume that a healthy money relationship requires having our financial house in perfect order. We gather our bank statements and bills and examine our debt load. We consider how our income and expenses balance. We anticipate contingencies and emergencies. We insure against catastrophes. We project how long we will work and make plans for retirement. We get sage advice about saving and investing. Step-by-step we execute our plan.

Wise planning eases some of the tension people feel about money. But it isn't enough.

With all that under way, we might consider our work complete. It isn't. Wise planning eases some of the tension people feel about money. But it isn't enough.

If we actually manage to get all of our financial

ducks in a row, happiness can still elude us, and there's a chance we might end up more uptight about money than ever. Moreover, even the most astute among us never reach a point where we don't regularly face crucial money decisions. It's a reality of our existence. It's the mode we will live in until the day we leave this constantly shifting world. Yet we have reason for hope. Even as we address our concerns, issues, and struggles, we can still develop a thriving relationship with money. That's a liberating message for all of us, especially if we deal with long-standing money difficulties. We don't have to be perfect to enjoy peace.

Let us give you a concrete example of what we mean. Financial professionals agree that hardly anything is more crucial for the well-being of an individual or family than paying down consumer debt—that is, most borrowing beyond a home mortgage, such as car loans or credit card balances. Consumer debt eats at us like cancer, with high interest rates translating into wasted money and added worry. But some solutions to destructive forms of debt can fuel the underlying problem.

There's a mentality that often drives debt reduction. It says, "Get out of debt and your life will be better." "Just do these easy steps and you'll be financially home free." "Go without now so you can accumulate more in the long run." "Don't spend now so you can spend later." But any solution that offers a quick fix to an entrenched problem reflects the consumer myth that we can have what we want when we want it. Any approach that subtracts something from our life without adding a better substitute just creates a craving for more. And the crazy idea that we should get out of debt now so we can buy more later feeds an unhealthy longing to acquire more when we already have enough.

Can we make this really practical? You might be reading this book while sipping a five-dollar cup of coffee, a daily habit that makes a larger dent in your budget than you want to admit. Maybe you're dressed in clothes you "paid for" with plastic. And perhaps you drive a new car to a job where your paycheck doesn't cover your bills. Something inside you realizes, *This doesn't add up*. You understand you need to change. So with fresh resolve you slice your spending right and left. You swear off your favorite coffee shop, shopping mall, and car dealer.

We want to suggest a different starting point: begin by adding more good stuff.

We agree with you that unhealthy habits indeed need to change. But we want to suggest a different starting point: begin by adding more good stuff.

By adding "more good stuff" we don't mean another round of spending. We're talking about leading with generosity grounded in grace. Instead of putting all your energy into cutting, focus on giving. Start by volunteering. Spend time helping family, friends, and strangers in ways that also give life to you. Consider giving to a cause you care about, some dollars you didn't give last time you saw a need. By leading with generosity you begin to quiet the gnawing hunger you thought you were satisfying by buying more and more stuff. Soon you will see the good results that come from an openhearted life. When you choose to live generously you break your persistent desire for more. And when that happens, it's far easier to get out of debt.

Those are the kinds of manageable steps we will coach you to take in the chapters that follow. We don't promise overnight, superficial success. We aim to lead you to long-term transformation through a new money mindset.

We aim to lead you to long-term transformation through a new money mindset.

We want you to remember that whatever money challenges you might face right now probably took a while to develop. They might take just as long to fix. In the meantime, as you work on your issues, don't let your balance sheet determine your self-worth. We want to tell you that God loves you whether or not you're buried in debt, and your family and other people love you too.

So humble yourself. At the same time you look to a financial professional for help, you might choose to seek out a pastor or another trusted spiritual counselor who will hear you where you are. Or as we suggested in chapter 1, open up to a small group of friends. Just find a way to be honest. We think transformation begins with discovering and admitting how our money mindset impacts us financially, relationally, emotionally, and spiritually.

The New Money Mindset Assessment

Because real change starts within us, we need to remake our hearts in order for new habits fully to take hold. It is often difficult, however, to have an objective view of what goes on inside us. To help us get an accurate view we worked with Thrivent's research and analysis team to develop the New Money Mindset Assessment™, a forty-eight-item tool to give you insights into your own thinking. In a moment we will invite you to go online and respond to this series of short statements. The tool takes about ten minutes to complete. The self-assessment isn't about how much money you have or don't have but about how you perceive your relationship with money. We think you will find it intriguing.

As a business leader and psychologist, we think that assessments—wisely used—reveal a lot about us. They can't tell us everything, but they can help us gain perspective. Thrivent's research team created this self-assessment specifically to help you discover your money mindset strengths as well as opportunities for growth.

We're grateful to internal Thrivent researchers who designed and tested the assessment. As they built this tool they focused on how *consistently* it would measure our money mindset (reliability) and how *accurately* the test would measure generosity readiness (validity). They used rigorous statistical techniques to uncover the best questions to gauge your money mindset and sought advice from renowned outside experts. More than 9,400 people across the United States participated in various stages of research conducted to develop this tool.[1]

The result is one of the most thorough and accurate assessments of a Christian's relationship with money that we know of. The inventory exposes some myths about money and will also show you how your thinking probably already lines up with some of what we believe are sound financial, psychological, and spiritual principles of a new money mindset.

So before you read the next few chapters, go online and respond to the forty-eight statements. You will immediately receive your score on four different money mindset continuums in order to determine where you are on the path toward a new and healthy relationship with money: the Freedom Continuum, the Community Continuum, the Contentment Continuum, and the Calling Continuum. Each score measures one aspect of your relationship with money. As you read the rest of the book, you can use your money mindset scores to help you discover how to improve your money mindset.

Taking the Assessment

As you take the assessment, keep these things in mind to get the most consistent and accurate results:

- Don't spend too much time on any one item.
- Go with your first response.
- Complete all the items.
- If at all possible, take the assessment in a quiet place.
- Be honest with yourself.

And have fun! This inventory is intended to prompt reflection and conversation. You will use the results to help you evaluate your strengths and challenges. If you are reading this book on your own, show your New Money Mindset score to someone who knows you well and see if that person agrees with your discoveries. Whatever your context, it should lead to some truly helpful insights for you.

Go to www.newmoneymindset.com/getyourscore to find the New Money Mindset Assessment.

After the Assessment

Now that you have taken the New Money Mindset Assessment, you will want to print your score output sheets and keep them handy as you continue reading the book. The chapters that follow will explain the importance of each continuum and the money attitudes each one measures. Your score and other feedback will help you look inside yourself to better understand how you view money, generosity, and the impact of your faith on both. Your results will give you clarity about your own next steps, detailing your strengths along with areas where you can grow into a new money mindset.

Find the New Money Mindset Assessment at www.newmoneymindset.com /getyourscore.

Your responses to the statements in the self-assessment will help you explore the heart of this book. As you read on, you will find four chapter pairs (4 and 5, 6 and 7, 8 and 9, 10 and 11). Each pair looks more deeply at our natural human longings as well as at new ways of thinking that equip us for a better relationship with money.

The first chapter in each pair looks at legitimate

desires that have the potential to lead to unhealthy attitudes and actions. We look at our longings for *security,* for *independence,* for *more*, and for *success*. The second chapter in each pair lifts up a biblical vision of how we can live and what that response looks like. We will find *freedom* and *community,* as well as *contentment* and a confidence in living our *calling.* We look at the self-assessment statements that point to healthy attitudes and suggest practical steps you can take to nurture those attitudes.

Your Money Mindset Adventure

The process of growing an openhearted life brings both struggles and victories. It's not something we ever perfectly attain. But it's an adventure we undertake in faith. A man we refer to as the "subway Samaritan" is a good example.

On a chilly January day, fifty-year-old Wesley Autrey and his two daughters—ages four and six—stood waiting on a New York subway platform when a man in his late teens began to have a seizure. Wesley and two other bystanders assisted the man as he writhed on the platform floor, unable to control his body as the electrical storm erupted in his brain. Eventually the man, film student Cameron Hollopeter, stopped seizing and stood up. He began walking in his own strength, but he started to waver to the left and right, back and forth. Before anyone could reach him, he fell from the platform onto the train tracks about four feet below.

When Wesley saw Cameron fall, he heard a voice: "You can do this. You are going to be okay."

Wesley immediately jumped onto the train tracks and tried to rescue the young man, who continued to seize. Unable to get a secure grasp on him to lift him out of harm's way, Wesley noticed the last thing anyone would want to see while struggling on a train track: the lights of a train heading his way.

Wesley called to some women above to hold tight to his two little girls as he covered Cameron with a full-body bear hug to contain his legs and arms within the rails.

Five cars flew over the two men as they lay between the tracks before the train finally screeched to a halt. As they lay motionless, the man kept asking Wesley, "Are we dead? Are we in heaven?" As Wesley later told an interviewer, "I gave him a slight pinch on his arm and said, 'See, you are very much alive.'"

Wesley called up from below the train to tell his children he was okay and waited for help to arrive. Cameron was taken to the hospital and recovered fully from his fall.

Wesley became a hero overnight, receiving many accolades and medals, and he was interviewed often about his heroic act. When asked why he jumped onto the tracks, he said, "The mission wasn't completed. I was chose [sic] for that." Wesley recounted how right before his feet left the platform, one specific moment flashed through his mind. "Twenty years before, I had a gun put to my temple; it was a misfire, so I was spared. I was spared for a purpose."

"You can do this. You are going to be okay."

Wesley had often thought about the gun that clicked without firing. *Why did God spare me?* he wondered. He believes he was spared in part to save Cameron Hollopeter. As he lived out his God-appointed mission he could trust that voice that told him, "You can do this. You are going to be okay."[2]

While God doesn't call many people to jump onto a subway track to rescue a stranger from an oncoming train, we do believe that he calls us to an adventure that can feel almost as terrifyingly risky. Growing into a new money mindset requires trusting God for our financial and personal well-being. He beckons us to a place of freedom, community, contentment, and calling. And to each of us he says, "You can do this. You are going to be okay."

CHAPTER 4

LONGING FOR SECURITY

WHEN I (JIM) WAS TWENTY-ONE YEARS OLD, I boarded a plane for the first time and headed to Africa for a summer of volunteering. Once in the air, I watched the wings buck up and down. I asked the passenger next to me if they were supposed to do that. "Yes," he assured me. "If they didn't flex they would just snap off"—a revelation that did nothing to ease my anxiety.

En route to Africa I stopped in Paris for less than twenty-four hours. I spent most of that time searching for my backpack, which had vanished in the baggage maze. Minus my clothes and other essentials, I climbed on a train to the south of France, where my mission trip would begin. When the sleeper car I had paid for was commandeered by a family gesticulating wildly while speaking in a language I didn't comprehend, I made the twenty-hour trip sitting upright on a wooden bench.

Fast-forward through two weeks of ministry among university students, when my backpack caught up with me just in time for me to change out of the clothes I had been wearing since I left home and move on to Morocco. After a couple of weeks there, I returned to France and hopped a plane to the West African nation of Cameroon.

Upon landing, I took an eleven-hour taxi ride into the Cameroonian jungle, packed into a Peugeot station wagon with eleven other people. My recovered backpack rode up top with several crates of chickens. I was instructed to sit on the lap of someone's grandmother. After fierce protests—by me—I complied.

As our driver played chicken with oncoming trucks, there were numerous times I feared I was about to die. The longer we drove, the farther I moved from what I knew as civilization. I soon left behind the land of electricity, telephones, television, and running water.

Not long after we had begun our journey, I prayed we would make a bathroom break. How naive of me to assume we might stop anytime soon. Or that there would be a bathroom. We stopped once—after five hours. At the edge of a very dense jungle, as the sky broke open in a torrential downpour, all of my fellow travelers stood or squatted to relieve themselves. Not accustomed to "relieving myself" in a mixed-gender, public chorus line, I couldn't go.

I felt an unfamiliar, unsettling sense of being a minority. Even in the capital city of Douala, I was the only white face in the crowd. I was different, and maybe I was somewhere I didn't belong.

Riding six more hours in the pouring rain, pressed flesh-to-flesh in the Peugeot with eleven strangers, feeling like an old man with an extraordinarily large prostate, was not what I'd anticipated as a young missionary. Still I believed that God had called me to serve in the remote communities of Cameroon.

That night, in a small African village, I was shown to a mud hut and climbed into a hammock that would be my home for the next six weeks. I listened to the rain pour down, drifting off to sleep under a thatched roof that kept me mostly dry.

Money Planning
Life often presents challenges that rattle our security. Sometimes what's at stake is a simple convenience. Or a soothing, familiar environment. At times life itself is at risk. As I ventured off to Africa, my desire for safety and security was healthy and normal. That longing is sensible and appropriate,

especially compared with its opposite, being so care-free and heedless of consequences that we're unwise about our surroundings or decisions.

When it comes to dealing with money, we believe that a completely carefree or reckless attitude is unwise. Kept in proper perspective, a desire for financial security can be healthy and normal.

For example, Jesus exposed the foolishness of a king who would go to war without calculating if he had everything needed to finish the job (see Luke 14:31-32). Jesus also painted an unappealing picture of a son who ran away to a distant country and squandered his inheritance on wild living, leaving himself so destitute that he craved the slop fed to pigs (see Luke 15:11-16). A potentially reckless king and a prodigal son would both benefit from a little money foresight, as do the rest of us.

Kept in proper perspective, a drive for financial security is healthy and normal.

People often think of financial preparation in terms of specific products they should buy to increase their peace of mind, such as obtaining life insurance to protect and provide for loved ones. But let's frame this in terms of some broader, long-term goals:

- It's wise to **pool resources to guard against circumstances that would devastate any one**

person. Generally this is done through insurance policies or noncommercial initiatives like church needy-family funds. Think of this as a modern method of sharing to meet one another's needs, as in Acts 4:34-35, where the early followers of Jesus pooled their resources for distribution "to anyone who had need." This principle applies to things like loss of property, income, health, life, and more. This type of planning builds a sense of reassurance and protects a person and his or her dependents from becoming destitute because of a single catastrophic event. The path to bankruptcy often begins with an unprotected risk that sets off a chain reaction of bad options.

· Another form of wise money planning is to **save personally for risks that can't be insured against** or where it would be hard to pool with others, such as a job loss or other significant unexpected expense. Most financial professionals suggest saving enough money for six to twelve months of regular expenses in an easily accessible, low-risk/low-volatility account. (An easily accessible account is one that allows you to get at your funds immediately without having to pay withdrawal penalties or sell an asset. A low-volatility account is one whose value doesn't go up and down dramatically. Stocks, for example, can be highly volatile, while bank CDs or savings accounts are generally low in volatility.) This emergency fund helps ensure that you have resources to ride out many of life's ups and downs. It might not be glamorous or have a big investment return, but it offers you personal confidence. You want to pool your catastrophic risk (see above) and put this emergency money in place before you do any other major saving or investing.

- Another wise step is to **save for expenses so that you don't have to borrow.** Most of us need to borrow (take out a mortgage) in order to buy a home, but it is best not to borrow to fund items like transportation needs, a down payment for a home, and educational opportunities. While borrowing lets us move ahead with a purchase before we have cash on hand, it also limits our future freedom. All borrowing puts us under the burden of repayment, which left unchecked can grow to crushing proportions.

- An often overlooked money tool is **learning how to give both generously and wisely.** The government offers tax incentives for giving, but these are often complicated and require forethought if we are going to maximize the benefits. It's also important to learn to contribute in a way that our gift doesn't do unintended harm to a person or organization. Think of a young person who receives too much money too soon. Or the ministry that couldn't manage a gift all at once or that was suddenly beholden to the giver. Or the organization where an endowment or estate gift allows the organization to stop innovating.

- Finally, wise planning allows us to **strategize and save for when we choose to or are forced to stop working for a paycheck.** As life expectancy continues to grow (babies born today are expected to live on average to 120 years old if trends continue[1]), planning for and managing retirement is critical so we don't burden others but instead remain productive in our callings, from volunteering and mentoring to being outstanding grandparents.

There is no doubt that setting out and achieving these goals help our sense of well-being. Do those priorities overwhelm you? Know that they are a lifelong journey; start now and build from where you are. If you feel you need professional guidance, a wise financial advisor will help you pull the pieces together within the realities of your current money situation.

Good Security

We long for security in part because we have a basic instinct to survive. Physical and psychological security are crucial to all aspects of human health and flourishing. For example, if as parents we are able to meet our children's basic needs and even some of their wants, they flourish, and we feel good. God has built us to want to be good providers and responsible stewards of what he has entrusted to us.

Creating "good security" motivates us. Yet sometimes that task becomes painfully difficult. Consider the parent whose spouse has passed away, and the remaining parent struggles to provide for their children. It's incredibly stressful. Or the parents whose child suffers with terminal cancer. Their world has been turned upside down, and they can't give their child what all parents wish for their children—good health.

I (Brad) remember a time when I was Christmas shopping with my wife, Sue, and our two young children. The store was wall-to-wall with shoppers, with the sights and sounds of Christmas everywhere. We were savoring the time together and the fun of Christmas gift-buying as a family. Suddenly, our happy adventure became a nightmare. Our five-year-old daughter, Melissa, had vanished. Both Sue and I frantically searched for our beloved little girl. All kinds of horrible fears raced through our minds.

Nothing mattered except finding Melissa and keeping three-year-old Matt safe as we searched. After what felt like an eternity, we discovered our daughter playing hide-and-seek in the clothing racks.

Perhaps you can imagine how it feels to be the parent of a lost child. Or maybe you remember being that child who wandered off, and fears and tears welled up until you were found. Our need for security is deep, real, and won't go away.

Take a more positive example of how feeling secure builds a strong foundation for success. Studies have shown that if students are laughing and having fun before an exam—that is, exhibiting behavior that suggests they feel secure and confident—they score higher than students who lack a sense of well-being. This is true whether the students have prepared well or not. Scores consistently go up when students at least *feel* secure before a test.[2]

Losing Perspective

Feeling safe is a good thing. However, as crucial as security is to our surviving and thriving in life, an unending quest for *financial* security can undo us. It causes us to lose perspective.

An unhealthy drive for financial security can lead to a scarcity mentality, which makes us feel compelled to gain more and keep more for ourselves.

We think there aren't enough money and goods to go around. But a surplus mindset says, I have enough for myself and enough to share.

We know many competent people who by every worldly measure have experienced exceptional success. They have all the possessions money can buy. And yet they remain driven by deep insecurity:

- A woman in Asia has palaces, chauffeurs, and private jets, but she never stops searching for some new travel experience to satisfy her unmet longings.

- A man nearing retirement with more than half a billion dollars never stops chasing more, because there is no finish line in the race to beat himself or his friends.

- A young American dot-com entrepreneur has more money than he could ever spend, but because he fears that others will take everything away, he won't allow seasoned professionals to come alongside him to help him grow his business.

In the New Money Mindset Assessment, we included statements that highlight several insecurities everyone feels to one degree or another. You may have agreed with one or more as you took the assessment.

Your Freedom Continuum score indicates whether you are closer to longing for security or living in freedom. Let's look at the statements that reveal the presence of a *disproportionate* focus on feeling secure, and in the next chapter we will look at statements that suggest the way forward.

An unhealthy drive for financial security can lead to a scarcity mentality, which makes us feel compelled to gain more and keep more for ourselves.

"I worry a lot about not having enough."
We might think this statement resonates only with people struggling to get by. Not so. On the fifth floor of Boston College's McGuinn Hall sit five hundred pages of responses from 165 super-rich households, the results of a study that asked people with assets of at least $25 million about their lives. These super-rich households averaged $78 million in assets, with a couple of families reporting net worth in excess of $1 billion. As the *Atlantic* quipped, "The survey's respondents are wealthy enough to ensure that in any catastrophe short of Armageddon, they will still be dining on Chateaubriand while the rest of us are spit-roasting rats over trash-can fires."[3]

But the Boston College study titled "The Joys and Dilemmas of Wealth" discovered that the survey respondents tended to be discontented. They worried about how their money affected their work, family, and other relationships. Despite those anxieties about the potential negative impacts of wealth, they didn't feel they had enough money, and most considered themselves financially insecure. These super-rich people believed they needed an additional 25 percent in assets to feel secure.

These super-rich people believed they needed an additional 25 percent in assets to feel secure.

One of the study's authors, Dr. Robert Kenny, concluded, "The research shows the rest of the world, who often think that if they just made one more bonus or sold one more item or got one more promotion, then their world and their family's world would be so much better, that this isn't necessarily true."[4]

Most of us recognize that a scarcity mentality can drive us to accumulate more money than we need, but this study suggests that having a lot of money can also produce insecurity. While the super-rich may illustrate the point most powerfully, we all get fooled into thinking that security is linked to wealth, at least to the tune of 25 percent more than what we have right now!

"I just don't have time to help others; I have enough trouble taking care of myself."

This statement might be true of people on the far bottom of the economic scale, but for most readers of this book, this statement suggests something else might be amiss. The issue might be more of a mind-set than a reflection of their actual money in hand.

What most people don't realize is that helping others can be a way of taking care of ourselves. A study referenced in an article titled "Twelve Ways to Keep You and Your Family Healthy" concludes that people who volunteer are on average 22 percent less likely to die during a span of four to seven years than others who didn't volunteer. The article quotes Hannah Schreier, a post-doctoral fellow at the Icahn School of Medicine at Mount Sinai in New York City, who asserts that helping others might lower our cardiovascular risk.[5] So even if you are barely surviving, you can still profit by giving yourself away when you have no other tangible resources to give.

"I find it difficult to live in the moment."

People overly concerned about security spend a lot of time thinking about the future. They focus on the countless things that can go wrong, or they imagine all sorts of tragic scenarios and how they might respond to them. They live in the future while they could be living for today and trusting God for tomorrow.

I (Jim) strive to live in the present. The reason I make it such a priority is that I am so tempted to live in the future. My job as a consulting psychologist for corporations and their leaders means I spend much of my time looking down the road several years and seeing what is most likely to happen. This is a great asset when I work with complex people and organizations, but that same strength becomes a liability when I get distracted into speculating about the future and fail to live in the present God has given me.

As a single father for nearly fifteen years, raising two daughters who wanted to be in the moment was sometimes a challenge for me. I was either getting ready for my next international business trip or just returning home from one. Young kids live in the present, and being there for them is crucial if we are to develop meaningful attachments with them. When the girls were in elementary school, I often suggested we go out on the lake to get away from all of life's pressures and pleadings. Today my university-age daughter and I keep up this practice in the form of "Dad-and-Daughter Dinners," time we have shared weekly since she started college four years ago.

"Having money helps me take control of my future."
"With enough money, I could make sure that life goes the way I want it to."
"I like to be in control."

These closely related sentiments are summed up in the final statement—the unhealthy desire for control. That's because it's so easy to start believing that a little more money will secure our destiny.

This can show up in an excessive desire to save or

a wish to have a really large bank account. We reason that if we have enough money for emergencies, we won't be affected by even the worst financial storm. But remember what we discovered in chapter 2. Attitudes of security or surplus are not linked to how much money we have in the bank. They are instead intimately coupled with our relationship to God. The size of our savings doesn't necessarily bring the security we long for.

I (Brad) remember the most difficult conversation I ever had with my dad as if it were yesterday, even though it happened twenty years ago. It was even more difficult for him than for me. It wasn't "the talk" about sex or dating. It was all about money.

The size of our savings doesn't necessarily bring the security we long for.

Sue and I were in our early thirties, with two little kids, a small house, and a dusty basement. We wanted to finish the basement and move the toys out of the living room. Frankly, I wasn't sure we could afford to get the job done. Sue had just chosen to stay home, and our income was cut by more than 50 percent. I was working for a company still in the start-up phase, so I felt nothing near financially secure. I figured that if I did the basement fix-up myself, we had just enough money. At least that's what I hoped.

Since my dad had built the house I grew up in,

he offered to come over and "supervise." Given my skills, he ended up showing me how to do my project. My dad was incredibly handy, but not all that talkative. Except that day! I could tell he had something on his mind but was having a hard time getting the words out.

We were laying tile in the bathroom. I was on my hands and knees; he was giving me good advice on how to keep the tiles straight. We were just about done when he finally said it: "I need to talk to you about money." I assumed I was going to get a rare lecture about borrowing money or something. I knew my dad had never borrowed a dime and was worried we were overextended.

His next words took me aback. "I'm going into the hospital for heart surgery next week," he said. "If I don't make it through, I want you to know about your mother's and my finances." This was a very difficult conversation. No lecture, but a peek into something he viewed as extremely private, something he had shared with almost no one else and clearly wasn't comfortable sharing with me.

I was worried. He was a teacher, and my mom stayed at home. So I knew they never made a lot of money. Finances always seemed like a burden to him. Only one good bit of news ran through my mind. I knew that my dad—a child of the Depression—was thrifty.

As my dad started laying out the facts and figures, the picture became clear. He had made all the right money moves, but it was apparent to me that he never felt secure, nor did he feel he could be as generous as he longed to be. For his whole life he had lived within his means and saved plenty of money. He wasn't rich, but he was prepared. Still, it was clear that even though my parents had done all the right things with their money, my dad had yet to gain a sense of security.

Overcoming Insecurity

It's really no surprise that any of us feel insecure. That nagging feeling comes in part from a lack of money know-how. It can also be rooted in a lack of trust in God. But the problem is also bigger than any of us. We live in a culture that exaggerates our need for security and safety.

Marketers in the United States spend about $200 billion a year on advertising, and making us feel insecure dominates their list of tactics. Take automobile tire ads. Who hasn't seen a happy family barely avoid a crash, saved solely by their good tires? The pitch essentially promises, "Buy our tires, and your loved ones will be safer in rain, sleet, or snow."

We live in the icy north of Minnesota. We take tires seriously. So why do marketers play on our fears? Because it sells. The reason advertisers appeal to our fears is simple. Todd Van Slyke, an advertising instructor at the Illinois Institute of Art–Schaumburg, says that these appeals "play on our inherent fears of the unknown or that something is going to kill us. This is why scare tactics are stunningly effective."[6]

Our own lack of knowledge, combined with our lack of trust in God, multiplied by the pressures of culture, make us easy prey to fear and insecurity. The nearly 50 percent of Christians in the United States who feel less than secure long for rest. We all want to escape our worries about money. But we need strategies that work. We will explore some of those strategies in our next chapter.

Feeling secure about money comes from planning. It comes from evaluating your real-world needs and doing the right practical things. But checking those off your list isn't enough. A sense of security deep down inside also comes from growing the right perspective. So we will focus on how we can overcome fear and embrace freedom, resulting in a more confident approach to whatever life throws at us. Remember, it's not about how much money we have. It's about embracing a new money mindset.

CHAPTER 5

LIVING IN FREEDOM

I (BRAD) WAS VISITING MY PARENTS and wanted to take them out for dinner. They liked a restaurant at a strip mall nearby, and I volunteered to drive. I had a general sense of where it was, and we headed off. But at the first left turn my mom said, "Brad, don't turn here. Go up and take the next right."

I was confused. I knew the restaurant was to the left. Why would she want me to go another block and turn right? As a good son, I did as I was told, and we took the next three rights before we finally arrived. When I asked why we took the roundabout way, my mom said, "I don't make left turns anymore. They're way too dangerous!"

Left turns aren't a problem for me, but they were for my mom. So she had made a significant adjustment in her driving habits. It helped her feel safe, even though it somewhat restricted her freedom in driving.

My mom made a wise change to dispel her driving fears, but when it comes to financial habits, fear is rarely a helpful place for us to manage from. Fear only amplifies our sense of insecurity and makes us feel less free.

Money Fears

Money fears arise when we have an uneasy sense about what lies ahead or when we see an already difficult situation becoming even more serious. This danger can be real or imagined.

At one extreme are folks whose fears are real and justified. They live paycheck to paycheck with no savings or too much debt and do face the risk of a financial mishap or worse. When my mom realized that turning left threatened her and everyone else on the road, she came up with a pragmatic solution to lessen the danger. Folks living on a financial edge similarly need to find ways to lower their risk.

Risk-lowering actions cause discomfort. They often mean admitting we have overstretched our incomes, requiring us to give up a lifestyle we like or even to start over. Knowing we are loved by God no matter what we have or what we do can help us muster the humility to ask for help. Not for one more loan to get us through or a favor from a family member or a friend, but *real* help: wise input and support to make changes in our own behavior. Taking action to build basic financial freedom can pay off in peace of mind, if not in lifestyle. Think of it like the driving analogy: for a time you might need to make only right turns. But it's better to adjust your habits than to cause an accident, injure yourself or others, or have your license revoked because of your recklessness.

On the other extreme are people whose money fears are more or less unfounded. At some point they realized that putting away money for emergency needs, for example, or to minimize borrowing makes them feel secure. Their good habits should bring them a sense of calm. But some savers don't know how to define "enough." They lose perspective and put themselves under constant pressure. They believe they are just being prudent, but some put away every last penny until their frugality sucks the joy from their life. They may grow stingy and reluctant to give. They make all the right money moves yet rarely feel peace. They work hard to feel free yet remain driven by fear.

Money is not the only resource we may hoard out

of fear. We might also fall into habits of protecting time and energy. Most of us have probably ignored calls to volunteer, for example, by telling ourselves our schedules are tight and others have more spare time. Or we might excuse ourselves from situations we anticipate will drain us, such as listening to an elderly relative who rarely stops complaining. These responses are rooted in a scarcity mindset, a fear that we don't have enough for ourselves, much less enough to share.

In this chapter we want to address the underlying insecurities that cause all of us to experience anxiety and dread from time to time, exploring how growing a relationship with God can calm our fears in a way that goes beyond our own efforts to create security. Then we want to suggest specific strategies for living in freedom.

A Rich Relationship with God

If we want to begin to break free from our fears, the first thing we should do is return to the simple but profound assurances of Jesus:

> I tell you, do not worry about your life,
> what you will eat; or about your body, what
> you will wear. For life is more than food,
> and the body more than clothes. Consider

the ravens: They do not sow or reap, they have no storeroom or barn; yet God feeds them. And how much more valuable you are than birds! Who of you by worrying can add a single hour to your life?

LUKE 12:22–25

Jesus understood clearly that faith and resources go hand in hand. He noticed how worries about our security tempt us to keep things for ourselves. In fact, just before Jesus gave the assurance quoted above, he told a parable about a rich fool who boasted about building bigger barns and filling them full so he could kick back

To break free from our fears, the first thing we should do is return to the assurances of Jesus.

and take life easy (see Luke 12:13-21). Despite his grand business ambitions, the man was the opposite of someone wise in managing his blessings. He ignored God as the real source of his security, instead relying on his wealth for a false sense of safety and control. Jesus called him a fool because he wasn't investing in a rich relationship with his Creator.

We face a similar scenario when the doctor speaks a diagnosis we don't want to hear. Or we get the phone call in the middle of the night that upends our world. Or a spouse announces he or she is leaving. At those times it doesn't matter how big our bank accounts are; they will not give the security we long for. Jesus says our security comes from the fact that God loves us. Our heavenly Father gets great pleasure in giving us his kingdom, both on earth and in heaven. He knows our needs and is gracious and generous toward us.

In Luke 12 Jesus provides two practical ways to invest in a rich relationship with God. First, he says, we should store up treasures in heaven by giving to those in need, the spiritual discipline of generosity (see verses 33-34). Choosing to be generous reflects our gratitude for all that God has given us. All of us are surrounded by countless needs. Some can be met by donating dollars. Others involve our hands. All require us to give our hearts.

Second, in the parable that comes next (verses 42-44), Jesus notes that servants who use the resources entrusted to them for the benefit of others, as the Master has asked of them, are the ones God praises. As wise stewards of God's gifts, we make a concrete investment in our relationship with him when we serve others with everything he has given us.

Investing in a rich relationship with God is the basic spiritual truth that grounds everything in this book. We think this is especially true if we want to develop a new money mindset.

Positive Practices

Of course it's not enough to say, "Don't fear" or "Stop relying on your own efforts to feel safe." We can't develop a sense of security by focusing on the negative. Putting all our energy into conquering what we fear won't work in the long run; more likely it will only fuel our unease. Our research suggests that people are more likely to enjoy a sense of freedom regarding time, energy, and money the more they buy into these positive statements:

> *Investing in a rich relationship with God is the basic spiritual truth that grounds everything in this book.*

- God meets my needs.
- I don't think about money unless it's running short.
- I don't often worry about the future. I take each day as it comes.
- I give to people in need, even if I barely have enough myself.
- I pray about the big decisions in my life.
- Deepening my relationship with God helps me feel peaceful about my future.

On the one hand, these attitudes are a gift from God, a sign of his transforming his children from the inside out. On the other hand, God has revealed specific strategies for deepening those attitudes. Let's look at two of these strategies, especially how they connect to the statements you responded to in the New Money Mindset Assessment.

"I pray about the big decisions in my life."
"Deepening my relationship with God helps me feel peaceful about my future."

Pause for a moment and think about the most unwise life decision you ever made. It probably comes to mind quickly, that time you look back on and wonder why you didn't make a better choice. It's okay. All of us have those moments, days, or seasons we look back on and wish we had picked a different path. Now consider this: the two statements we call out above can change your approach to your next major decision and to every choice after that.

These statements fit together naturally. They both point to a rather obvious strategy: prayer. Focusing on prayer—one very concrete way of deepening our relationship with God—can bring wisdom and peace as we make decisions. God knows everything we need before we ask. But we don't. Prayer not only recognizes God's power to supply our needs but gives time to let his wisdom rule.

Listen to Jesus on this subject:

Ask and it will be given to you; seek and you will find; knock and the door will be opened to you. For everyone who asks receives; the one who seeks finds; and to the one who knocks, the door will be opened. Which of you, if your son asks for bread, will give him a stone? Or if he asks for a fish, will give him a snake? If you, then, though you are evil, know how to give good gifts to your children, how much more will your Father in heaven give good gifts to those who ask him!

MATTHEW 7:7-11

Jesus teaches us several things in this short passage.

First, *God is a loving heavenly Father*. He cares about us even more than the best earthly parents care for their children. Spending time in prayer with God reminds us of this core reality.

Second, *God is a provider*. He has the power and the desire to give us what we most need. That doesn't mean that he promises to make us rich or to give us piles of possessions if we just ask him in

Prayer not only recognizes God's power to supply our needs but gives time to let his wisdom rule.

faith. This is the falsehood of the prosperity gospel, which teaches that if we are faithful to God he will unfailingly bless us with wealth—and if we don't attain affluence, the blame falls on us for somehow failing in our faith. Instead, Jesus promises that God is able and willing to supply us with "good gifts." In the parallel passage in Luke, Jesus says more specifically that God will give the gift of the Holy Spirit (see Luke 11:13). The point is that God will give us all we truly need to thrive. The more we pray, the more we're able to believe in this bedrock truth.

Third, *Jesus encourages us to pray for anything we think we need.* God is not just loving and powerful; he also seeks a relationship with us. Our insight into what we need might be limited, like a child who can't see why he should pay attention in school, make friends with vegetables, or go to bed when his dad or mom says so. Sometimes we might ask amiss, but God cares enough to keep providing for us.

We believe these are the facts we each need to live into: by praying to our heavenly Father, we deepen our relationship with him. When we deepen our relationship with the good God who is ultimately in charge of our lives, we begin to feel more peace. And the more God's peace fills us, the more readily we turn to prayer to let God guide our decisions in every part of life. The cycle is really that simple.

Developing a regular and meaningful life of prayer—yes, that is a lifetime task. If you decide you need to deepen your prayers and your dependence on God, there are many resources available. Consider the many great books on prayer that can help.[1] Churches offer classes on prayer and opportunities to pray with others. Your pastor can give you guidance.

The most practical thing you can do as you consider choices, big or small, is simply to stop and pray. In the heat of the decision, you might even need to walk away. Ask God for wisdom and take a few minutes to listen to the Spirit. If peace doesn't rule your heart, then wait. And if you still lack clarity, ask a friend to join you in praying and listening.

Praying for Real Needs

Years ago I (Brad) was working in Minneapolis for a Lutheran organization that provided loans and other planning services to churches. Sue and I had just moved our family to a house we hoped would be home for a long time. Life felt good. Settled. Then I heard I was on a list of candidates for a position within our larger church body in St. Louis.

I felt honored to be considered. But we really didn't want to leave the Twin Cities. Besides being fresh off a move, we were surrounded by great friends, and we knew no one in St. Louis. Even so, Sue and I started praying, separately at first. My initial prayers were, *God, is this what you are calling me to do? Me? Why me?* Then they were more like, *If it is your will, make it clear to me. Really clear!* Before long, Sue and I began talking to God about it together. We were in a small circle of friends and neighbors, and we asked for their prayers and prayed as a group.

One day Sue and I said out loud for the first time, "We're moving, aren't we?" It wasn't anything specific, just a sense of peace we both had from God. The job paid far less than I had been making before I started working for a Lutheran body, but that wasn't a big part of our conversations or prayers. We accepted that we would adjust our lifestyle to fit what God wanted us to do. We had saved enough that we could follow his call unafraid.

When the hiring process dragged on, we thought we must have been wrong. The offer that came months later felt like it was out of the blue, but by then we had complete agreement about the change we hadn't wanted. And so we moved.

Prayer lets us speak our requests to God and take time to meditate on his direction. Praying through our money decisions often creates a space for wisdom and insight to enter a process in which emotion and desire might otherwise take the lead.

The God Who Meets Needs

The following statements are closely related and best summed up in the last.

"I don't often worry about the future. I take each day as it comes."

"I don't think about money unless it's running short."

"God meets my needs."

How do you become a person who really counts on God?

Faith that God meets our needs grows best when nurtured by his powerful Word.

The Bible is, if nothing else, a record of how God repeatedly met the needs of his people. He gave Abraham his promised son. He lifted Joseph from slavery and made him Pharaoh's right-hand man. He rescued Israel from oppression in Egypt. He instructed his people to take special care of the most needy in our world, including widows, orphans, and foreigners among us. And fast-forwarding to the New Testament: God came to us in Jesus Christ, who forgives our sins and offers us life eternal, with a final promise to make a new heaven and earth. The God of the Bible meets the needs of his beloved people, although not always on our time schedule.

Faith that God meets our needs grows best when nurtured by his powerful Word.

The theme of God's faithfulness runs all through Scripture, but it is especially thick in the psalms. Here is a typical verse: "Great is your love, reaching to the heavens; your faithfulness reaches the skies" (Psalm 57:10). The more you are immersed in Scripture, the more you will naturally do what the psalmist does: "I will remember the deeds of the Lord; yes, I will remember your miracles of long ago. I will consider all your works and meditate on all your mighty deeds" (77:11-12). Seeing and recalling God's faithfulness in Scripture trains our hearts and minds to notice more and more of his faithfulness in our lives today.

When we're confident in his faithfulness, it can dispel our fears. Before I (Jim) set out on my mission trip to Africa, I had to raise $4,000 to cover my travel and living expenses. In addition to sending an appeal letter to family and friends, I worked at a large drywall construction company to earn enough for my college tuition and to pay for the portion of the trip expenses that the mission agency expected me to cover. I wouldn't be allowed to go on the trip unless I had 100 percent of the $4,000 in contributions. Each day I kept checking the mail to see if someone else had responded to my appeal letter, but I had pretty much run out of friends and relatives who hadn't already sent me money.

For several weeks, nothing arrived. I began to

think I wouldn't be making the trip. With three days to go, and on my last day of work, I was $400 short of my goal, and I had no way to come up with the rest of the money.

I had been driving the company dump truck all day, sweating on the plastic seats, going back and forth between a commercial job site and the city dump. Being hot and smelly from loading and hauling trash only added to my discouragement about the trip I had told so many people about. As I pulled the dump truck into the company lot and slid out of the cab, I saw someone walking toward me. I had never driven a dump truck before that day, so I was pretty sure I had done something wrong and was about to hear about it.

That wasn't it at all. The company owner approached me and said, "I heard from one of the guys that you're going on a service trip next week to Africa. I became a Christian last year, and I want to give you this to help you with your trip."

My first reaction was relief that I hadn't wrecked the truck. I thanked Mr. Kastner and walked away, tossing the envelope in my lunch box. I didn't bother to open it, thinking it contained at most maybe twenty-five dollars. That would have been a generous contribution back then—especially for a college kid you didn't know who did mostly grunt work.

I drove home tired, sweaty, and despondent. I

walked into my parents' house, dropped my lunch box on the counter, and slumped in a chair at the dinner table. My mother, as always, asked me how my day was. I told her I got to drive the dump truck, and then I headed to the mailbox to see if any more support money had come in. Meanwhile, my mom opened my lunch box and found the unopened envelope inside.

"What's this?" she said when I returned.

"It's a check I got today from Mr. Kastner for my mission trip."

"How much is it for?"

"I don't know. Probably fifteen or twenty dollars."

She encouraged me to open it. You might have guessed by now that inside that dirty, crumpled envelope was a check for $400. I was flabbergasted and thankful. In that moment God's promise of provision became entirely real.

Generosity Disciplines

We won't suggest that God will in every instance take care of our needs like this. Nor do we think that if we only have more faith, we will get more blessings. Hardly. During that last day of fund-raising, I didn't have much faith at all! But we do think this example illustrates the teachings of Jesus and of the psalmist—that we can trust God to care for our needs, whether for body, soul, or spirit. It's crucial to remind ourselves of those scenes in our lives when we knew God was faithful.

We have found that healthy, biblical attitudes toward all we possess become embedded in our lives when we consistently practice certain spiritual disciplines like prayer. But there are also "generosity disciplines" that can help as well.

One summer when I (Brad) was in high school, our church youth-group leader challenged us to participate in a spiritual-formation small group. It was loosely based on John Wesley's "Great Experiment." For forty days we would practice five disciplines:

1. Every morning awake at 5:30 and spend thirty minutes reading and reflecting on the Bible.
2. Every evening spend thirty minutes in prayer and confession.
3. Each week fast one day from sunup to sundown—about 5 a.m. to 9 p.m.
4. Each week meet in community to encourage one another.
5. Each day do one completely unselfish, generous act for someone else.

When we all signed on, we assumed the most difficult disciplines would be getting up early on summer break and fasting. And at first those disciplines challenged us most, but as summer wore on, they became more routine. Surprisingly, the generosity discipline became the most challenging.

This act of kindness was supposed to be done in such a way that we would get absolutely no benefit from it—no favor in return, no recognition, not even a thank you. The deeds needed to be as completely selfless as we could make them, modeled on Jesus' saying, "Do not let your left hand know what your right hand is doing" (Matthew 6:3). We discovered it was hard not to have our actions benefit us. One of the first things I did was to wash the dishes after dinner without being asked. My parents were so struck by my simple act of service, they handed me the car keys to go hang out with my friends!

The generosity discipline isn't just for high school students or for a summer. We can all undertake this practice. You may want to undertake a forty-day generosity discipline challenge during the weeks leading up to Easter or some other time of year when you choose to focus on spiritual growth. To start more modestly, you could do one act of selfless generosity each week. We would encourage you to make this about more than giving—even *not* to let giving be an option, unless parting with money particularly challenges you. Something about having to *do* something for others shapes us even more than giving cash, although that, too, is an important discipline.

Even small acts of generosity help us discover that it is more blessed to give than to receive (Acts 20:35), and as you become accustomed to these small acts, you can consider doing something more deeply sacrificial.

Back to Freedom

Trusting God for all we need helps release us from the bondage of fear and worry. The apostle John said it this way: "There is no fear in love. But perfect love drives out fear, because fear has to do with punishment. The one who fears is not made perfect in love" (1 John 4:18). Put simply, our most vital step in overcoming our fear is to put our trust in the One who created us, loves us, and sacrificed himself for us, and who sustains us daily as we invest in a rich relationship with him.

When we shake off fear and worry we become free to give ourselves to greater things.

Easy to say, not always easy to do. Yet the practices we suggest here go a long way toward helping us put our security into God's hands. And that leads to an entirely new level of liberation.

When we shake off fear and worry we become

free to give ourselves to greater things. To God. To family. To friends. To those in need. As long as we are wound up in worry about money, we won't give ourselves wholeheartedly to others, because our always-pressing concern remains on us and our problems. Once we trust God for our present and future, we can let that go. We can begin living without worry and therefore live in freedom with and for others.

CHAPTER 6

LONGING FOR INDEPENDENCE

EVERY WINTER FOR THE LAST TWENTY-FIVE YEARS, I (Jim) have drilled several holes in the ice of a nearby lake to make sure it's thick enough for skating. I'm not reckless. I want to make sure I know how thick the ice is before my kids and I go out on it. I observe weather patterns, such as how low the temperature drops and for how long. Past experience offers a time frame when the lake should freeze solid, but that can vary widely from year to year. Friends from warmer climates think I'm insane to "walk on water," and I watch with amusement as some visit the lake and walk a few yards onto the ice before scurrying back to land. To be honest, there is no perfect way to test the ice except to venture out, drill in hand, and see for myself.

When it comes to my own generosity habits I intentionally endeavor to nudge myself out on the ice, all the while knowing I can let go of fear because my strong God upholds me. I'm especially inspired by watching people who give more of themselves than I do. When I ask what energizes their giving, they help me discover my own unique ways to extend myself. They move me beyond my usual limits.

Lately I have been practicing stepping out in faith without calculating what generosity will cost me, instead of holding back when I have already dispensed "enough." My goal is to meet the needs I see without doing the math on what portion of my time, energy, or money my giving represents. I aim to do what I feel called to do, trying to rise above worrying whether I will have enough. Not because I have a mountain of inexhaustible reserves—I don't—but because God knows my needs.

Daring Generosity

We want to introduce you to a variety of people who have proven their readiness to step out onto the ice. They are just a few of our real-life heroes. They lead with generosity, living out the money mindset that they have enough for themselves and enough to share. Their unique ways of giving not only meet real needs but build deep connections to the people around them. They are:

- **A ninety-one-year-old woman** who never married but saw every child as her child, every family as her family, and every need as her need to meet. Raised on a farm, she taught school for thirty-five years. Her overflowing love for Christ caused her to give herself in Christian service full time for many months at a stretch for the next thirty years. Until the day she died, she was a generous volunteer.

- **A pastor and recovering alcoholic** whose day in, day out routine mirrors the Good Samaritan. He's always ready to stop to help a stranded motorist in the rural community where he serves, ever willing to stay up all night at the bedside of a dying hospice patient, and never too busy to listen to the challenges of his friends and family.

- **A retired couple** who could afford a big resort house in a warm climate but instead chooses to live in a modest house in the city so they can give scholarships to kids who need a hand up. They get to watch their generosity in action, and they are among the happiest people we know.

- **A neighbor** who visits an elderly man each day to make sure he is okay and to take care of his needs. This neighbor says his giving makes him feel blessed. The elderly man's family thinks he is a saint.

- **A single dad** whose income dropped drastically during the height of the world financial crisis of 2008. He kept volunteering with his kids and giving 10 percent of his former income while trusting God to provide for his family. Several friends said he was foolish, but giving while earning next to nothing brought stability, wholeness, and family cohesion in the midst of a terribly difficult time.

- **A young family** with two children, one of whom suffers with a severe neuroskeletal disease. They truly live as though their lives are not their own. As they serve the world around them, the family exudes a joy that emanates from a conviction that everything belongs to God.

- **A successful businessperson** in the thick of his career who every day for more than a decade has taken time to write ten to twenty personal thank-you letters to his employees. He has become one of the most beloved leaders in his company.

- **A twentysomething** who quietly cleans up the church every week after everyone else has gone home. He describes it as his way of giving to God and his community because he doesn't have a lot of financial resources to share right now.

These friends all have something in common. Not only have they received back more joy than they could ever foresee, but their various ways of giving have helped strengthen connections between family, friends, neighbors, coworkers, and strangers. Their willingness to give in daring ways has extended and deepened community.

We all know that the good feeling we get when we write a check is only half the story. Anyone who has ever pounded nails at a Habitat for Humanity build knows what we are talking about. So does anyone who has baked and delivered a loaf of bread to a person too frail to leave home. And if you have ever been on the receiving end of someone demonstrating love to you by sharing their bounty, then you know the fullness of life together. It's in relationships that we experience the joy of generosity.

It's in relationships that we experience the joy of generosity.

Earn it and keep it, and you will find yourself wanting (whether "it" be time or money or talent). Manage it wisely and then share from your resources, and you will know firsthand the blessing of life together. While our resources can give us a certain kind of independence, they can and should do so much more: they can also create a healthy interdependence.

Listen to this proverb from the Hebrew Scriptures: "Generous hands are blessed hands because they give bread to the poor" (Proverbs 22:9, MSG). The circle of gift and gifted, benefactor and beneficiary would not, could not, exist without both halves of the circle. Being generous is one of the best ways we experience life together, and connectedness can't happen if we wall ourselves off from others. Making the circle of peace larger and the banquet table of grace longer is the essence of what Christ has called us to.

Gaining Independence

Within each of us resides a longing to stand on our own. We feel it almost from the first days of life. With each passing moment, we move from relying on parents and caregivers to satisfy our every need to squirming away to explore the world. As we grow up, we struggle to form and express our own perspectives and to do things our own way. We ache for opportunities to make good and bad choices, to decide for ourselves whether we succeed or fail. And we know that something is amiss if we don't eventually break free from home and strike out on our own.

To become fully functioning adults, we must grow up and get along in the world of real responsibilities, accountabilities, consequences, and rewards. Put simply, there are some things you have to do for yourself. These markers of healthy independence also happen to enable you to be generous:

- **You need to brush your own teeth.** Taking care of your body, God's temple, allows you to live more generously. Minding your physical, mental, and spiritual health often goes hand in hand with generous living.

- **You need to wash your own car.** Caring for your worldly possessions is good stewardship. Good stewardship allows you to have more for others. Here's a deep thought: by consistently caring for the things you possess, you will be more free to honor the things you can never possess, such as relationships, the present and future, and life's unexpected events, both good and bad.

- **You need to do your own homework.** Feeding your mind and boosting your knowledge across your lifetime equips you to add value at home, work, and church. Cultivating a hunger to learn will give you the opportunity to share generously with family, friends, neighbors, and others the wisdom you gain in your studies, in Scripture, and in the school of life.

- **You need to confess your own wrongs.** Part of being an independent adult is the ability to say, "I'm sorry." Pride keeps you from flourishing. Humbly recognizing your limitations opens doors in a world that often slams them in your face. Admitting, "I was wrong" earns you more credibility than pointing out, "I was right."

- **You need to possess your own faith.** Developing a life of faith requires discipline and at times sacrifice. By nurturing your relationship with God, you take responsibility for your spiritual maturity. No one can do that for you, and your daily journey with the Savior will produce a life rich in gratitude, service, and wonder. You will never regret the time you spend with Jesus.

We hope your caregivers in early life set you on the path to mature adulthood and to doing these things only you can do. Accepting these responsibilities allows you to carry your own weight in a tough world. They're really essential to survival. But independence taken to an extreme robs us of the help and joy that comes from community.

Independence and Interdependence

The Community Continuum in the New Money Mindset Assessment reflects the struggle to balance independence and interdependence. We yearn for more money so we can be appropriately independent—so that others don't have to support us with their own hard-earned income. But we often end up allowing money to make us imagine that we don't need other people, at least as much as we did when we didn't have as high an income. For some, the more money they make, the more they become disconnected from others emotionally and psychologically.

Christians who have been financially poor can be uniquely vulnerable to this phenomenon. Missiologist Donald McGravran coined the term "redemption and lift" to describe what happens when poor people meet Christ, quit bad habits, commit to the virtues of hard work and strong families, and as a result begin to accumulate wealth. Their newfound success more often than not distances them from their old life and friends. Unless they intentionally stay engaged, they lose interest in the needy people who face the same material and spiritual deprivation they once did. The result of gaining wealth is that the wealthy have a harder time empathizing with people who suffer economic woes—the very ones Jesus tells us to care about the most.

I (Brad) am part of an effort to plant a church in an urban area of St. Paul, Minnesota. It's a second-generation church plant from a suburban church, and now Sue and I are part of this effort to begin something new. At first we were a neighborhood Bible study hoping to be a church plant, but now we feel like we have launched. We intentionally located the church in an impoverished urban area. Why? The people need to hear about Jesus, yet they live on the edges. They are less likely to participate and give. The people most likely to be able to help live in the suburbs and aren't interested in coming into the city, possibly because of fear or just the hassle factor. So we intentionally landed in a very urban area. It's interesting. It's just fun. And being in that community bridges a gap that would inevitably grow if we didn't constantly choose to close it.

Sharing Stuff

While we long for independence, we can't escape the fact that interdependence provides security (spiritual, emotional, physical, and financial) in a way we never can enjoy alone. Many of the statements on the self-assessment address an unhealthy drive for independence. We will first look at a few of our challenges, and then in the next chapter, some ways to move forward.

"I don't like to let people use my stuff."

"It's hard for me to accept help from others."

I (Brad) was raised in an upper Midwest neighborhood. My dad, a teacher, lived alongside a bricklayer, small-business owners, a professional football player, a plumber, a doctor, an engineer, and a pastor. Some houses were bigger than others, but not by much. When the doctor's family purchased a color TV, the whole neighborhood was invited to watch it. It was many years before my parents sprang for a color television, but in that neighborhood we could all go to the doctor's house to sample the new technology. Today's affluence makes it harder to live together in community.

Affluence makes it harder to live together in community.

When we can afford the luxuries of life, we don't need to invite each other into our homes to share a special possession. With each passing day, our rugged individualism grows ever more rugged, and even the brand names of our stuff are telling—there are no wePhones, wePads, wePods, or weMacs.

Many people are convinced that flourishing happens in groups of one, where thriving means, I am doing well all by myself. Our culture tells us that if we stack up enough money and possessions, we don't need to depend on others. And the lie goes on by suggesting that this is a good thing, which we re-inforce with sayings like "I don't want to be a bur-den to my family"; "I can take care of myself"; "I don't need the government's assistance"; and "God helps those who help themselves." There is truth in each of these ideas. But they become dangerous when they undermine our ability to live in community.

The reality is that sooner or later we all come to a place of need where our own resources aren't enough. We know a young married couple who are a good example of this. They were just getting started. Both had jobs, and together they had medical insur-ance. Then their young daughter became seriously ill, and strained finances meant making tough choices. They suddenly faced desperate need.

When someone at their church heard of their plight, the congregation sprang into action. They sponsored a fund-raiser to pay uncovered medical bills and lavished emotional support on the family as well. When the crisis subsided, the woman met with volunteers who led the fund-raiser. She shared how she and her husband had tried so hard to become "independent," but they had hit a wall. They were thankful to have visited a church and found people who would help them even though they didn't know them well. She concluded, "Now I understand what both mercy and the church are—thank you!"

"I would rather be alone than have to listen to other people's problems."

"I need a lot of lead-time when it comes to scheduling things with family and friends."

In itself, independence isn't a problem. As we have said, we want our children to be independent, and for good reasons we value healthy adult independence. Parents feel like failures if their adult children continue to come to them every time they make a decision. Couples don't want their partners to cling to them or become overly needy. We rightly admire people who strike out on their own and find success.

But healthy independence turns bad in small and subtle ways. The signs that our drive for independence has become unhealthy are many and varied, depending on the context we're talking about. We see them crop up in our relationships, for example, as described in an article titled "Signs That You're Too Independent for a Relationship":

- Your friends and family constantly accuse you of never listening to them.
- You make decisions first and ask for feedback second.
- The thought of hearing someone's advice about your situation makes you angry.[1]

Other signs might be:

- You find it increasingly hard to ask for help, for directions, for assistance.
- You mostly want to be alone and hardly ever want to be with others.
- You enjoy having friends but find it annoying when they start sharing their troubles or problems with you.

In other words, a big red flag of an unhealthy sense of independence is when we start feeling like people are a bother!

"If I had a lot of money, I wouldn't answer to anyone."
A recent study demonstrates this point objectively. University of Minnesota professor Kathleen Vohs conducted an experiment that showed how the simple presence of money in a room shapes people's behavior. For example, when money—even Monopoly money—is in the environment:

- People become less helpful to others.
- People work hard and want to achieve goals *on their own*.
- Painful experiences don't seem as painful.
- People don't mind being socially excluded.
- People see social inequalities as acceptable.

"In all of our experiments," Vohs told a reporter, "people who are reminded of money are really good at pursuing goals, but they're not that interpersonally kind or warm. They're kind of standoffish, keeping in their own head, not interested in being friends with anyone."

Vohs added, "So what you get are high-motivated people who are not very socially sensitive." Not antisocial, she clarified. "Antisocial suggests things like they're actively pushing people away. It's more like they're siloed."[2] Like the silos that dot the Midwest rural landscape, each structure is tall, imposing, and somewhat beautiful, but not connected to any other building. People arrange themselves the same way. They often use their possessions to isolate themselves. They end up standing alone and self-contained.

As much as we long for independence, the Bible declares our need for one another. It even recognizes the tension between the need to do things for ourselves and relying on others. In his letter to the people in Galatia, the apostle Paul introduces a thought that at first sounds confusing, if not contradictory. He writes, "Carry each other's burdens, and in this way you will fulfill the law of Christ" (Galatians 6:2). A few verses later he says, "Each one should carry their own load" (verse 5). While the meaning would have been immediately clear to the original readers, it's lost in most English translations. The words translated *burden* and *load*, which are similar in English, have distinctly different meanings in the original Greek in which Paul wrote. The "burden" we are to help each other lift is literally a boulder too large for any one person to shoulder. The "load" each of us is to carry alone is a Roman soldier's daypack.

In everyday life we sometimes have difficulty distinguishing between a "load" an able individual should carry and a "burden" that requires help from others, but the point remains obvious. Independence must be balanced with interdependence.

Everything from family life to public policy to church ministries with the needy would be easier if we perfectly understood where personal responsibility ends and group responsibility begins. But we can start by admitting that only in community can we recognize and deal with our blind spots and live more fully in the light. This is nowhere more true than in our efforts to be generous.

Creating Community

Last March, I (Brad) was doing some regular Saturday work along with Sue at Urban Homeworks, a ministry in north Minneapolis that rebuilds homes and neighborhoods to provide quality housing for income-qualified residents. At the heart of the effort that day was a young construction trainee—working on his GED, learning how to supervise a crew, pulling together people from city and suburbs and beyond to get an important job done.

It was supposedly spring here in the north, and all the snow had melted, but then we got hit with a big snowfall and cold snap. The house we were working on had no windows, and the day's goal was to install some. Since Sue and I don't consider ourselves skilled construction labor, we went out front to work on a Dumpster almost the size of a school bus.

Independence must be balanced with interdependence.

The overgrown trash bin had stood in front of the house for weeks, and it had been filled by neighbors far and wide with used mattresses. All of them had to be emptied so the bin could be loaded with recyclables and actual construction scraps. So our job was to first shovel snow out of the Dumpster and then haul all the dirty mattresses to the back of the house for trash pickup. The one good bit of news was that the bedding didn't smell because it was all frozen.

Digging and dragging was cold, hard work that made me wish I had a hammer and a younger back. In the back of my mind, I was thinking the problem wouldn't exist if people had taken responsibility to dispose of the mattresses properly. But the bigger purpose that day was to get a house fixed from the ground up for a new family, and dealing with the Dumpster was a must-do step.

What constantly amazes me is how a project like this brings people together. Over the past twenty years, Urban Homeworks has put 17,000 volunteers to work, supervised more than 1,200 construction trainees, and provided homes to 400 urban neighbors. It's a type of ministry replicated by fabulous groups all across the country.

We were all just part of the team getting our hands dirty. There was no us and them, no rich or poor, no commentators arguing that people should rely on themselves and pull themselves up by their bootstraps. What got built that day was more than a house. It was a community of redemption and celebration. It's a microcosm of the interdependence of people who see themselves as citizens of God's kingdom. Despite all of our longings for independence, it's where we want to head. Next we will talk about how we can get there.

CHAPTER 7

LIVING IN COMMUNITY

A LITTLE-KNOWN FOREIGN MOVIE lets us glimpse the best of what it means to share community. In the lovely French film *My Afternoons with Margueritte* (*La tête en friche*, 2010), Gérard Depardieu plays an easygoing but nearly illiterate simpleton named Germain. This bulky, aging man grew up unwanted at home and bullied by his mother, teachers, and classmates, who considered him stupid. As an adult he has nothing beyond a hand-to-mouth existence in a house trailer close to his elderly, crass, alcoholic mother, who loathes him more than ever. He supports himself with odd jobs and by selling vegetables he grows in his small garden.

One day Germain visits his lunch spot, a park bench where he has named nineteen pigeons he considers his friends. There he meets a very properly dressed elderly woman, Margueritte, who spends her days reading Camus, Proust, and other French classics.

As Germain and Margueritte continue to meet day after day, their friendship grows. Germain shares his pigeons' names, and Margueritte introduces him in the gentlest manner to the joy of reading. Slowly she teaches Germain the beauty of the written word and the great thinkers. When near the end of the movie Margueritte is all but abandoned by her family and unable to see clearly enough to read her beloved books, Germain rescues her from a nursing home and brings her to live closer to him. He becomes her reader, and together they continue their journey of interdependence as his sight overcomes her blindness, and her blindness opens his eyes.

My Afternoons with Margueritte illuminates the biblical call for us to live together in ways that make burdens lighter and lives richer. This very human tale lays bare how generosity—giving out of a surplus mindset—leads to a happy ending. As the psalmist wrote, "Generous gets it all in the end" (Psalm 37:22, MSG).

Built for Each Other

The Bible's vision for life together can be found in so many places, it's hard to know where to begin. Well, not literally. If we go to the first pages of Scripture, we see God's design for community right from the start. He brings the first human couple together. Children arrive on the scene. Families become great lineages. Communities grow. Peoples and nations arise. As the human story unfolds, it's obvious that the best and worst qualities of humankind show up when people gather in groups, but even our failings don't detract from the beauty of God's intentions. In fact, as soon as sin and death appear, God begins to reveal a plan of global redemption.

At the end of the Bible, we see *We are designed* "a new heaven and a new earth" *for community.* where all God's people gather in the New Jerusalem: "Look! God's dwelling place is now among the people, and he will dwell with them. They will be his people, and God himself will be with them and be their God" (Revelation 21:1, 3).

Between this beginning and finale, we see example after example of God's intention for us to live together in community, from his bold formation of Israel as a nation to the unleashing of the church. It seems we are designed for community.

Recent research reinforces this truth. In one study, consumers in thirteen countries were asked what they would give up for a year in order to keep Internet service. Nearly 75 percent of Americans said they would skip fast food. Eighty percent said they would forego satellite navigation, and an almost equal number said they would abandon alcohol before giving up the web.[1]

Many reasons must underlie this passionate attachment, but surely one of them is that people crave the connection the Internet enables. That's why social networking platforms—currently Facebook, Twitter, Instagram, and whatever springs up to replace them—rank highest in how people spend their time online.[2] There are limits to how much the Internet can connect us with others, but a sense of community is surely one of its draws.

The community God desires for us isn't just a feel-good thing. It's incredibly practical. A passage in 2 Corinthians shows that clearly.

At the time Paul wrote this letter, Christians in Judea were near starvation from a severe famine. On his journeys across the Mediterranean to start and visit churches, Paul repeatedly reminded new Gentile believers of their bond to the mother church in Jerusalem. This wasn't a history lesson or nostalgia. Paul raised an urgent need for financial gifts that would alleviate hunger in Jerusalem.

In his letter to the Corinthians, for example, Paul

praised the generosity of the churches in Macedonia to spur more generosity from the Corinthians:

> Brothers and sisters, we want you to know about the grace that God has given the Macedonian churches. In the midst of a very severe trial, their overflowing joy and their extreme poverty welled up in rich generosity. For I testify that they gave as much as they were able, and even beyond their ability. Entirely on their own, they urgently pleaded with us for the privilege of sharing in this service to the Lord's people. And they exceeded our expectations.
>
> 2 CORINTHIANS 8:1-5

The biblical vision of our life together isn't just emotionally satisfying; it's also highly practical. Let's see how this biblical ideal ties in to statements on the Community Continuum of the New Money Mindset Assessment and explore a couple of practical steps toward community.

"I don't mind when friends stop by uninvited."
"Most weekends, I end up helping a friend or family member with something."

The self-assessment uses the language of "friends" and "family" to talk about our closest ties. Our attachment to these dear ones makes sense because God has put them in our lives. We are naturally drawn to spending time with them and helping them.

For the Christian, there is an additional community, the church. It becomes an extended family, an intimate assortment of friends who share faith in Jesus. While there are abundant reasons to connect to a church, one rises near the top: so that we learn how to live together with others, even others unlike us. The great professor, novelist, and apologist C. S. Lewis put it this way:

> When I first became a Christian, about fourteen years ago, I thought that I could do it on my own, by retiring to my rooms and reading theology, and I wouldn't go to the churches and Gospel Halls; . . . I disliked very much their hymns, which I considered to be fifth-rate poems set to sixth-rate music. But as I went on I saw the great merit of it. I came up against different people of quite different outlooks and different education, and then gradually my conceit just began peeling off. I realized that the hymns (which were just sixth-rate music) were, nevertheless, being sung with devotion and benefit by an old saint in elastic-side boots in the opposite

pew, and then you realize that you aren't fit to clean those boots. It gets you out of your solitary conceit.[3]

The main purpose of joining a church, of course, is to give yourself more fully to God and grow in his grace. But deep companionship with other believers is absolutely essential to our spiritual growth. There is a reason Jesus joined "loving God" with "loving neighbor" when he talked about the two greatest commandments (see Matthew 22:37-40). If you want to break out of your siloed existence, participating in the authentic community of the church does that without fail.

Some people loudly protest this point. Their run-ins with the church have involved anything but community. Some have felt judged. Others find religious talk irrelevant. There are all sorts of reasons why some people become frustrated with the church. They all reveal one reality: the church may be a divine institution, but it is also a human one—meaning at times it's still thick with sin. If church has given you a bad taste or worse, don't give up on church as a whole; that would be like swearing off eating because you once got food poisoning.

Failure to connect is a key reason many people think church is pointless. That truth should move us not simply to attend worship gatherings but to commit to being active in a smaller group in the church: a choir, a class or missional activity, or a home group that meets regularly. Organized small groups of six to twelve people meeting in a home for prayer, study, and conversation can be found in almost every church, especially larger ones. All of these examples of church involvement are what we mean by "living in community."

Failure to connect is a key reason many people think church is pointless.

Bonding with other small-group members helps us experience grace. Meeting regularly helps us see that no family, marriage, or job is perfect. A group can provide not only encouragement but a sense of perspective that comes from being in on others' real lives. And feeling more connected to others makes most people feel closer to God.

There's an unexpected benefit to community when it comes to growing a new mindset on how we share our time, energy, and money. Connecting with both God and others opens us up and frees us to be more generous with what we have. When we watch others act from a surplus mindset, sharing ourselves becomes easier. And when we do things like welcoming new guests, we let others in and poise ourselves to help them. This openheartedness is indeed generosity in action.

"I give back to my community."
"In my neighborhood, we help each other out when someone needs a hand."

It's crucial to develop relationships with people who share our faith. It's just as vital to reach out to people in need, followers of Jesus or not. Developing connections in our community is another of the "generosity disciplines" we recommend. It naturally results in stronger community, whether we define that as a neighborhood or something bigger.

A dozen years ago, Peter and Cary Bolstorff took a bold step toward feeding the homeless of St. Paul, Minnesota. For some time they had supported local soup kitchens but felt God calling them to do more. And so the dream of building a mobile food kitchen was born. Twelve years later, Peter and Cary, with the help of many others, have served more than 400,000 meals to St. Paul's homeless population.

Mobile Action Ministries (MAM) is a not-for-profit, 100-percent-volunteer-operated organization bringing healthy, dependable meals to children, women, and men who lack the resources to eat regularly. This service has become more and more vital as government food-assistance programs continue to be cut. As other services dry up, a mobile food ministry like MAM fills the void.

Peter and Cary Bolstorff committed the time,

energy, and resources to lead a group of volunteers to do more than they could ever do alone. Meals are prepared, served, and cleaned up by small teams—often families—who make their way into the inner city to be Christ's hands and feet in action. Independence gives way to interdependence.

I (Jim) have found that my regular involvement over several years with MAM's food truck continues to remind me that the walls between people aren't nearly as high as I tend to think. After serving a meal, we climb out of the truck and talk to people. Some come from situations I can barely begin to imagine, even after difficult points in my own life as well as a long career as a psychologist, where I hear people's stories and offer them a safe space to pour out the worst hurts of their lives. I meet some who are as well educated as people who fill our businesses and boardrooms, and I hear how their lives took a bad turn. Any of them could just as easily be in our place. Or we in theirs. Breaking boundaries and meeting actual people on the street helps me remember that the act of living is inherently risky, and none of us can survive, much less thrive, without practical and spiritual grace from others.

A couple of years ago, I was serving lunch on a cold November day along with my daughters, Mira and Asha, to a large crowd of the city's homeless. On that particular day, besides handing out lunches from the mobile food kitchen, we were distributing clothing to anyone in need.

At one point a man named Sam rolled up in his wheelchair and asked if we had any blankets. He wanted to keep his lap and legs warm while he sat in his wheelchair. Sam told us he had just been released from a prison-based drug-rehabilitation program, and he hoped to make a trip to visit his children in another state.

We were sorry to tell Sam that the ministry didn't have any more blankets available that day. In the back of our car, however, was a blanket that had been handmade for me many years before. It was the blanket my girls and I picnicked on when they were young.

None of us can survive, much less thrive, without practical and spiritual grace from others.

They had played on it in the front yard of our home countless times. For many years I had cared carefully for that blanket, and it held special memories for me. The truth is, I didn't want to give it to Sam. So I acted like it wasn't there.

The girls knew otherwise. They began asking me if we should part with the blanket so dear to all of us. Finally they both said, "Let's give it to Sam, Dad." And so we did. It was the right thing to do, but I'm pretty sure I wouldn't have done it without my girls' encouragement.

When we reach out to the underserved and others in our communities, we end up not only helping them but stretching ourselves. The act of being generous with our time, energy, and money—and sometimes with our treasured personal possessions—helps us learn how to be even more generous. In an instant we find ourselves shifting to a surplus mindset whenever we let go of our earthly needs and trust God to provide for us just as we have provided for others.

Gathering and Scattering

"The best way to do ourselves good is to be doing good to others," wrote Thomas Brooks. "The best way to gather is to scatter."

Brooks was just twelve years old in England when the Pilgrims set sail for Plymouth, Massachusetts, in 1620. It's doubtful that as a boy he knew the wayfarers who set forth from his homeland, but in his later years as a Puritan minister he would certainly have grasped the concept of setting ourselves apart for the sake of faith, as the Pilgrims did. His words remind us of the generous patterns of the Native Americans who fed William Bradford and his band of English faithful.

"The best way to gather is to scatter."

Long before Europeans arrived in the Americas, indigenous people practiced a breathtaking tradition called the "Give Away." In the 1800s it was banned at the urging of misguided missionaries and others who believed it showed a lack of respect for private property. But the revived practice continues among some Native Americans to this day, done with tremendous care and grace.

Most early Americans were nomadic people. They needed to carry everything they owned either on their backs or on a travois pulled by a horse or a human. In that culture, there was no advantage to having lots of extraneous belongings. They would only hinder their owners along the way. You can imagine that each and every possession had to be held in high esteem if a traveler were to keep it and carry it everywhere he or she went.

The Give Away ceremony required people to carefully and thoughtfully go through their prized possessions and select which they would give to those they loved. These items weren't throwaway articles, because the nomads wouldn't possess any throwaway articles. They would instead be items that brought joy and pleasure through their utility.

A modern adaptation for your life might go something like this. At a time when you are about to experience a special event—a graduation, a wedding, the birth of a child, or starting a new job—you make preparations for your Give Away. Rather than receiving gifts from those who attend your special day, you give to those who have honored you with their presence. And you choose those gifts from among your most treasured possessions.

The thought of giving gifts to guests might bring to mind the extreme gift bags sent home with guests at children's birthday parties. Or maybe you can't imagine giving something to every person who attends a wedding or even a dinner to celebrate a new job. But you can adapt the Give Away to fit your life. The gift need not be expensive, but it should be significant. You might not be able to honor everyone present with a gift, but you could give to those most helpful on whatever journey brought you to your special day.

Among Native Americans, the gift might be a piece of jewelry or a prized hand tool or a work of art. Today as in past ages, a treasured wool blanket would be a cherished gift. The essential element is that the gift be chosen and presented with generosity and love. The end goal is to show and grow your connection with someone you want to honor, to celebrate and increase your shared experience of community.

Generosity Now

Like Thomas Brooks, Native Americans understand the brilliant truth that to gather, we must scatter. So how could you apply the idea of the Give Away to your everyday life, your Sundays through Saturdays? How ready are you to scatter what you have been blessed with in terms of time, energy, or money?

Remember the verse we shared in chapter 2: "The world of the generous gets larger and larger; the world of the stingy gets smaller and smaller" (Proverbs 11:24, MSG).

When we act with generosity, our world expands; when we succumb to stinginess, our lives shrivel. Do you believe that? We do. Again and again we have been challenged to choose between living open-heartedly or tightfistedly, and whenever we have resisted our natural desires and chosen to act with generosity, we have seen our relationships, work, and overall contentment expand.

Both of us are stingy by nature. Our parents and other elders who grew up in the post-Depression era taught us the phrase "We can't afford that." Deeply ingrained in our sensibilities is the desire to hang on to "my" stuff for a proverbial rainy day. But we have also discovered this: whenever we tighten our grasp, we invariably lose our grip.

Whenever we tighten our grasp, we invariably lose our grip.

The belief that we genuinely "own" our possessions is simply an illusion and a lie. That's why we find the idea of the Give Away so compelling. Jesus said more than once that the lilies and birds should be our example. They don't fret about their existence. They own nothing. Yet they contribute an awesome beauty to everything around them. Who among us can say that about our lives?

So what have you gathered? What are the things you believe you possess? Is it your home, your vehicle, your education, your income, your children, your reputation, or your health? All of these matter in carving out a pleasant existence here on earth. But how can we really own or control them? How would it help us to regularly give away something of great value to us? Can we think of a better reminder that everything in this life is transient than making a habit of parting with some of our earthly stuff? And how can we use that process to deepen our connections and community?

Billy Graham once said, "If a person gets his attitude toward money straight, it will help straighten out almost any other area of his life." British philosopher Bertrand Russell is quoted as saying, "It is the preoccupation with possessions, more than anything else that prevents us from living freely and nobly." And Martin Luther King Jr. said, "Every man must decide whether he will walk in the light of creative altruism or in the darkness of destructive selfishness."

Here are some next steps to try as you seek to use all that you have and are as a means to interdependence.

First, *what about your possessions?* Ask yourself if you agree with this quote from Thomas Brooks:

"The best way to gather is to scatter." Do you believe that? Take three minutes to write down your most-treasured possessions. Stuff, not people. Three minutes. Go!

What's on your list? Often we end up acquiring more than one of something that we value. Take computers, for example. Many of us have computers that run just fine but that we have relegated to the basement because we purchased something newer and faster. While that particular computer might not have been on your list, your new Mac laptop might have been. What if you took that somewhat dated computer down to a local resource center and helped them get it up and running? Or maybe computers aren't the best example for you. How about a watch you never wear? Could you sell it on eBay and give the money to a homeless shelter? What about clothing? Who do you know who needs clothing for work? Or where could you donate it that would make it available at an affordable price? What other things could you part with that would enrich someone you know?

We don't know about you, but we both have possessions in good working order that we never use. And slowly but surely we're trying to wisely move them along to someone who needs them more. We live in an age where many people could profit from these slightly used possessions. Are you willing to scatter what you have, both your favorite things and the things that are no longer your favorites?

Second, *how about your time?* Where could you give your time most impactfully? Think for a moment about ways you have volunteered in the past. Where are your skills and gifts most powerful? Listening to someone in pain, cooking meals for a family with a new baby, driving someone to a doctor's appointment are all ways you can give away your time, a very important "possession."

Third, *what about your money?* We don't assume that if you're reading this book, you have piles of cash to give away. In fact, we recognize that you might be looking for a solution to significant challenges. Money might be tight. It's just that plain and simple.

A generosity mindset says that it isn't the size of the gift but rather the spirit of the gift that matters. Think of it this way. If you give a silver dollar and a fifty-dollar bill to a four-year-old, which of the two objects will make him happier? The shiny, large, heavy silver dollar. If you make that same gift to a forty-year-old, which one would he hold on to if asked to choose? The dull, thin, light fifty-dollar bill. The same gifts have different meaning and value to people in varying situations. The same can be true with our financial gifts. Give what you have where it matters most. Don't judge your gift by some external system but by the impact of giving well. All you need to do is offer it up. The only true way to fail in this generosity movement is by not trying at all.

Make a gift today of your possessions, time, or money—or all three. Do it at a level you can afford. See how it reshapes how you feel both emotionally and spiritually, and trust that your gift well given will benefit the recipient. When we develop a mindset of thinking about sharing what we have with others, we begin to experience the joy of living in community.

CHAPTER 8

LONGING FOR MORE

I (Brad) get more than a little crazy when I hear the word *sale*! I'm lured in by a potent mixture of desire combined with opportunity and savings. The moment I think I'm getting a great deal, I lose all common sense, and I'll buy just about anything marked 50 percent off.

At my first job out of college I discovered that in the world of work at that time, wearing a coat and tie was obligatory for just about every male with a desk job. I decided the first day that I needed more than the one suit my parents had bought for me. Besides that lone suit, my wardrobe consisted of jeans and

T-shirts that had seen me through four years of higher education, plus a few white shirts and ties from my job bagging groceries. Clearly I had no idea where to buy a suit. I asked around.

One of my new coworkers told me about a shop not far away that sold suits at a big discount. It sounded like the perfect place for me! At the store I spotted exactly what I was looking for: *the sale rack*. Nothing hanging there was even mildly eye-catching. Nothing was my size. But when something is marked down, those issues are mere details. I picked a suit close to my size, a brown pinstripe that was the best of the worst. I honestly didn't think it looked too bad. I should have known otherwise when the salesperson tried to talk me out of buying it. But I had found such a good deal, I was undeterred. In the end, the alterations cost more than the suit, but at least I could say I had purchased my first suit on my own.

I didn't wear that suit for long. My parents saw it and were horrified—so aghast that they bought me another suit and threw in a sport coat. Given their frugal streak—which I inherited—you can guess how bad I must have looked. I would like to say I learned my lesson, but as I write, I am wearing a pair of shoes I also purchased on sale. I'm confident they will feel comfortable when they eventually stretch out.

Basic Needs

At the most basic level, there is nothing wrong with wanting more. Jesus himself says, "I have come that [you] may have life, and have it to the full" (John 10:10). The quest for abundance—for ourselves and others—is a healthy human instinct. When I went hunting for a suit, I knew I had gone to school to acquire skills that would help me make a living for myself and someday provide for others, and I was ready to take on the world, brown pin-stripes and all. Longing for a better life, to improve ourselves and our family's circumstances, and to leave the world better than we found it are all parts of how God made us.

Work is not only one of the means God uses to give us the good things we need, but labor itself is a gift from him. Every new day is a chance to be good stewards of our time and the talents he has built into us, and our labor gives purpose and meaning to our lives. What is more, the work we do to satisfy our material longings isn't a burden we simply endure until we can retire. In fact, the kind of retirement where we cease from all work to chase only leisure isn't a biblical concept at all. The apostle Paul instructs all followers of Jesus to do "something useful with their own hands, that they may have something to share with those in need" (Ephesians 4:28).

We both believe so strongly that basic human longings reflect legitimate, God-given needs—and that we should be part of helping people who face difficulty satisfying those longings—that serving the underserved has been a standing part of our lives for years. What we call the "generosity discipline" of service isn't an abstract ideal we entertain within our minds. Nor is it a warm feeling we keep tucked away inside our hearts. We make service-in-action an essential part of our schedules almost every week and often significantly more, setting aside time to serve the needy in our communities through organizations like Urban Homeworks, Mobile Action Ministries, and many more. What could be more basic than sharing the hope of Christ by helping create affordable, safe, peace-filled housing? Or ensuring that the poor have enough to eat? Our efforts are based on our recognition that all people have essential needs that deserve to be met.

All people have essential needs that deserve to be met.

Getting More

Sometimes the longing for more, however, can quickly turn into lust for acquisition. Human beings so easily take this beautiful gift and twist it. If our world today seems nearly mad with consumerism and materialism, constantly craving more and bigger and better, this is nothing new. Three thousand years ago, the writer of Ecclesiastes struggled with this relentless longing:

I said to myself, "Come now, I will test you with pleasure to find out what is good." But that also proved to be meaningless. "Laughter," I said, "is madness. And what does pleasure accomplish?" I tried cheering myself with wine, and embracing folly—my mind still guiding me with wisdom. I wanted to see what was good for people to do under the heavens during the few days of their lives.

I undertook great projects: I built houses for myself and planted vineyards. I made gardens and parks and planted all kinds of fruit trees in them. I made reservoirs to water groves of flourishing trees. I bought male and female slaves and had other slaves who were born in my house. I also owned more herds and flocks than anyone in Jerusalem before me. I amassed silver and gold for myself, and the treasure of kings and provinces. I acquired male and female singers, and a harem as well—the delights of a man's heart. I became greater by far than anyone in Jerusalem before me. In all this my wisdom stayed with me.

> I denied myself nothing my eyes desired;
>   I refused my heart no pleasure.
> My heart took delight in all my labor,
>   and this was the reward for all my toil.
> Yet when I surveyed all that my hands had done
>   and what I had toiled to achieve,
> everything was meaningless, a chasing after
>   the wind;
>   nothing was gained under the sun.

ECCLESIASTES 2:1-11

Most people believe if they had just a little bit more, they would be happy. Research suggests otherwise.

A few years ago, economist Angus Deaton and psychologist Daniel Kahneman of Princeton University discovered an amazing fact about the relationship between money and happiness. After analyzing responses from 450,000 Americans polled by Gallup and Healthways in 2008 and 2009, they concluded that day-to-day happiness in America doesn't rise once people have a household income of more than $75,000 per year.[1]

The study found a correlation between lower incomes and higher stress and dissatisfaction in life—up to a household income of $75,000. At that point, the authors suggest, people probably have enough expendable cash to do things that make them feel good, like going out to dinner with friends or splurging on some other treat now and then. But from that point upward, making more money doesn't make people happier.

As it turns out, it's not the actual amount of money—$75,000—that is so important. More important is where people rank in relation to the wealth of those around them. At the time of the study, $75,000 was 1.5 times the median household income in America.

Day-to-day happiness in America doesn't rise once people have a household income of more than $75,000 per year.

Research indicates a similar phenomenon and ratio in societies around the globe. Apparently being in the richer half of the population—even only by a little— has great value to most everyone, yet being way above the median (and carrying the weight that comes with it) has diminishing return.

Does that dollar amount shock you? It's so much lower than what many people think of as life-changing wealth. It's nothing like winning big in the lottery. Or getting adopted by a Warren Buffett or Bill Gates. It's far less than what media and marketers imply we need to feel like the world is our oyster, or whatever else we're into.

Don't we assume that we would be considerably happier if we just made twice as much as everyone around us? Or wouldn't we be turning cartwheels if we made many multiples of that? Perhaps if we made millions upon millions, we would feel bored with wealth and the trifles it brings, but most of us want to try it for ourselves. But $75,000 sounds so unextraordinary. True, as an annual income it's no small amount. Yet many two-income families bring home as much. Mastering a trade or combining a college education with the right job makes that number attainable for more than a few individuals. And yet research says that having more—acquiring all the things and experiences money can buy—doesn't make us any happier.

This empirical finding agrees with biblical wisdom, and it explains why so much in Scripture cautions about the dangers of wealth. On the one hand, God loves the poor and doesn't want them to remain poor. On the other hand, excess wealth doesn't better the lot of people who possess it. The writer of Proverbs sums up the balance nicely when he says, "Give me neither poverty nor riches, but give me only my daily bread. Otherwise, I may have too much and disown you and say, 'Who is the LORD?' Or I may become poor and steal, and so dishonor the name of my God" (Proverbs 30:8-9).

More and More

Striving for more begins as a healthy human instinct to meet our needs. It can enhance our lives financially, relationally, and emotionally. But our culture has taken this drive to an extreme. The trick is in knowing where to stop. Once again, it seems as if our human nature doesn't naturally know when enough is enough. And so we keep chasing after "more" through people, things, money, education, or whatever seems to work for us.

This is why Jesus warns against letting our desire for more run wild. He says, "Take care! Protect yourself against the least bit of greed. Life is not defined by what you have, even when you have a lot" (Luke 12:15, MSG).

Greed in any form can do us in. In particular we have observed two things that get people in over their heads: *square footage* and *number of wheels*. How big is your house? And what vehicles do you drive?

Homes in America are ever expanding. In the 1940s the average American house stood at around 1,200 square feet. The US Census Bureau reports that by 1983 the average new build was 1,725 square feet. In 2013 the average new home measured 2,600 square feet, the largest ever.[2] Of course the hazards of a home aren't just sheer size but everything we "need" to fill a bedroom for each child, a home office, entertainment spaces, backyard decks and gourmet barbecues, and

Two things get people in over their heads: square footage *and* number of wheels.

that increasingly popular third garage stall. Lacking a third stall makes a house what real estate agents call "functionally obsolescent."

For many of us, the endless quest for more and bigger and better probably involves something besides an overblown Starbucks habit; it's not that if we simply don't buy $5 coffee we will be fine. No. The reality is we might need to relocate to a smaller home and make more basic transportation choices. Why? Housing and transportation costs are the expenditures that put virtually everyone who struggles with money into the danger zone. Unfortunately, our expectations and actions around those major purchases are much harder to change than choosing to brew cheap coffee at home.

Like the writer of Ecclesiastes, we all struggle with consumerism and materialism, and the Contentment Continuum in the New Money Mindset Assessment highlights attitudes that point to this. Once again we will analyze the problem before we turn in the next chapter to solutions.

"Money can buy the important things in life."
"Deep down, I wish I had some of the nice things that other people have."

These two statements go hand in hand: we usually want the nice things that others have because we have somehow come to believe those things matter.

I (Brad) had my first experience with this temptation when I was in high school. Each day after classes, I had to walk from school to work—about a mile and a half. After work, sometimes I had to walk home—another couple of miles. I occasionally had access to our rusted-out Monaco station wagon or our family car, a Ford Pinto. These automobiles didn't reflect the image I wanted to convey to my classmates. Those legendary vehicles were so ugly, my friends still laugh about them decades later.

I had a vision of myself in a much better car. A muscle car. I was thinking that even a well-used Dodge Charger would send the message I was looking to convey: cool.

My dad and I made our way to the bank in one of our rusted-out cars. After filling out paperwork for a loan, we waited in the lobby. My stomach was spinning because I was unsure I would qualify. It seemed like forever before the loan officer finally appeared.

"I'm sorry, Mr. Hewitt," she began. "Your loan has been denied."

I asked why. She told me my mortgage was too large.

As soon as the words left her mouth, she realized something was amiss. What was the likelihood that the suddenly deflated teenager in front of her had a mortgage? She excused herself and went back into her office.

She soon emerged to tell me there had been a mix-up. Another person with the same name was applying for a car loan as well. Between his mortgage and my income, there was no way they were going to approve the loan. With the error cleared up, the loan officer told me my loan was approved.

Fast-forward two years. I had successfully paid off the principal and interest on my car loan, a feat I could rightly be proud of. But my Dodge Charger was fast becoming a bottomless pit for all of my extra cash, and my bank account was empty. This was right at the time when I was about to graduate from high school, and I had no money saved for college.

That simple decision made two years earlier at the bank significantly impacted the next phases of my life. My choices about where I would go to school were severely limited by tuition costs, so that I could no longer simply look for the best school I could get in to. Even at a lower-cost school, I would need to work almost full time to pay for college, which made it more difficult to soak up all that college offered both academically and socially. It was my first lesson in the pitfalls of "leveraged acquisition"—even though I did look pretty cool driving the car.

"Sometimes, I buy stuff I don't really need and then regret it later."

When I (Jim) was a graduate student with next-to-zero disposable income, I stumbled on an amazing classical guitar shop.

I had played guitar since I was a young boy, and at the time I owned a perfectly good classical guitar for someone of my ability. This shop had a beautiful ambiance. It smelled of Spanish cedar wood. The walls were lined with instruments made by Spain's most famous artisans and sold to some of the world's foremost guitar players. What could it hurt if I played a few of the instruments? I wasn't going to buy, just look.

Two days later, I was the proud owner of a very expensive guitar. As a recent college graduate, I had just acquired my first credit card and was proud that I had qualified for one. It was a Visa card from the Bank of Hawaii, which made me feel even cooler. These were the days of 21 percent interest, and I soon realized that my $650 guitar would cost me well over $1,000 before I could pay it off. At age twenty-five I had my first encounter with a credit card debt I couldn't pay at an interest rate I couldn't afford. For me this was the beginning of a hard life-lesson.

I knew when I bought the guitar that I couldn't afford it. But buying it was so easy. I knew what my dad would have said had he been there, but he was a couple of thousand miles away in Minnesota. I even remember feeling that I wasn't particularly credit-worthy. None of that stopped me.

When I took my new guitar home, it didn't really feel like it belonged to me. I couldn't play it in the way it was intended to be played. I had purchased the instrument out of a sense of insecurity, wanting to be like the world-class musicians. The melodies emanating from that guitar never felt true until I finally paid off the debt more than a year later.

"I don't spend as much time with my family and friends as they'd like me to."

I (Brad) made a significant career shift some years ago in part because of an uncomfortable incident that reflected this statement. I experienced a painful reality check about dividing time between work and family.

I was working long days and often evenings in a company based in the Twin Cities. I was getting plenty of affirmation for my work, and we all hoped the company would go public in a few years, bringing additional financial success to both employees and investors.

Then one week my wife, Sue, had to be away from home. When it came time for me to take over parenting duties, she said to Melissa, our five-year-old,

"Honey, I am going to be gone, and Daddy is going to take care of you."

As soon as Sue told our daughter that I would be her caregiver, Melissa replied without hesitation, "No, Mommy. I don't want you to do that. I don't feel comfortable around Daddy."

I feel awful admitting now I was a bit nervous about caring for my own five-year-old, but at the time I did think I could figure it out. Our daughter's words not only took me by surprise but cut me to the core. Clearly I wasn't the only one anxious about my ability to provide care for my daughter. She was even more upset. I had been working too much, and the result was a child who didn't feel at home with her daddy.

I'm not proud of that story, but it shook me up and helped me to change my course before it was too late. After this incident, I made an effort to spend more time at home. When it became clear I couldn't manage that well, I finally took a different job. It paid considerably less but didn't require as much travel. It was one of the best decisions I ever made, and we never missed the extra money.

Something Isn't Right

Across the years we have heard countless stories from women and men who feel trapped in an extreme longing for more, like a young engaged couple we know. Mark and Maria are both in their late twenties. If you could meet them, you would recognize both as quality individuals from wonderful families, and they both have degrees from good universities. One is an elementary school teacher, the other a business analyst for a midsize manufacturing company. But Mark has already accumulated $90,000 in debt. That might sound over the top, but the average undergraduate student-loan debt has more than doubled in the past eight years and now nearly tops $21,000. Many couples start life together with significant debt. They are so worried about survival that it feels impossible to think about generosity, whether of time, energy, or money.

Until debt becomes unmanageable, many couples don't learn the sad truth that no matter the size of the house, SUV, income, or influence, it's human nature to feel like we should have more. Part of that comes from simple greed. But part of the problem is that deep down we feel as if we won't measure up—to our parents' expectations, our family's hopes and dreams, or our own sense of self-worth—if we don't have more. So we try to get more and keep more, whatever it takes.

Most of us don't want to become materialistic, although many of us suspect we already are. We all experience temptation to be greedy, no matter how much or how little we earn, because greed is a matter of the heart and not of income.

How do we know when we have become inappropriately acquisitive? What signs tell us when longing for more has us in its clutches? We see signals much like in other areas when our life is misaligned. In Jim's thousands of hours as a clinical psychologist, he notes that some of these signs of misalignment or disconnect might be:

We all experience temptation to be greedy, no matter how much or how little we earn.

- dropping the ball—failing to do things you have promised to do
- strained relationships—because you aren't spending enough time on them
- financial commitments you can't keep— like getting behind on bills
- being unable to live within your "emotional means"—finding yourself sad, depressed, or anxious more than normal as a result of extending yourself unrealistically

As you think about these signs, you might notice a couple of things. You may be spending hours and hours surfing Amazon or other sites looking for some item you are convinced you really need. Or you may find yourself daydreaming about the next purchase that would really be nice to have. Or you might be wallowing in self-pity because you can't enjoy some object or experience others are enjoying.

As we have said, there's nothing intrinsically wrong with wanting to improve the quality of our life and enjoy the goodness of God's creation. But we have to look hard at the reality that our human nature is tempted to turn these good gifts into mere idols. Instead of supplementing and enhancing our love of God, they replace it. When that happens, we obsess over our possessions in ways that lead to the disconnect demonstrated in the four trouble signs. These symptoms point to a deeper problem of consumerism and materialism.

Because we live in a culture rich in material goods, we can be sure we will face this struggle our whole lives. There is no sense in beating ourselves up, as if we are the only ones with this failing. This malady strikes most people in modern first-world countries. That isn't an excuse to just give in to materialism, but it might help us to not despair or feel alone when we find our hearts corrupted by inappropriate desires. We can instead learn from the wisdom of the writer of Ecclesiastes—or in this case, his lack of wisdom. He tried everything—parties and wine, women and song, houses with big pools and gardens, and to top it all off a giant bank account. As he put it, "I denied myself nothing my eyes desired" (Ecclesiastes 2:10).

Yet in all the lists of things he tried, never once did he say he did something for someone else or acted with generosity or kindheartedness. The writer concluded that "all is vanity," and his words ring true when we make life solely about ourselves, because our greedy longings are never satisfied.

Materialism and consumerism endanger us because they promise pleasure to the eye but can never satisfy the heart. Generosity is the best diagnostic tool for greed, and it's also the best prescription. Let's turn to some practical strategies that can help us better manage these desires for more.

CHAPTER 9

LIVING IN CONTENTMENT

MY GRANDPA COLBY (Brad speaking) was a young teen when he was summoned to a neighbor's farm to help milk a less-than-cooperative cow. Apparently the farmer was off on a drinking binge and had abandoned the cow for days. She was miserably full of milk and unwilling to let anyone touch her.

As Colby arrived at the barn and moved toward the unhappy cow, he must have sensed her tension. He talked to her as he approached and grabbed the milking stool. But when he knelt down to milk the cow, she lurched forward and kicked him in the leg, opening a deep gash. His torn flesh bled severely.

There were no modern ambulances or helicopters to come to his rescue, so getting him to medical attention took precious time—lost time that allowed his young muscles to die from lack of blood. In the end, in order to save his life, his leg had to be amputated.

Colby had ventured down the road toward a neighbor's farm to perform an act of kindness, not realizing his life would change forever. As I grew up and more fully understood my Grandpa Colby, what struck me was that he wasn't in the least consumed by his past. I never heard him tell his story firsthand; I had to piece it together from family recollections. He never thought it necessary to tell me how he felt about losing his leg. The grandpa I grew to know could have been bitter about the drunken farmer or the call to take responsibility for someone else's animal. Yet he never complained about his bad fortune or the fact that the situation left him without a leg. Instead he stayed focused on the future and the abundance of good things he could do—like catch fish with his grandkids and beat me at checkers!

Having the use of two healthy legs is surely a "possession" many of us believe is necessary to enjoy a full, happy, and large life. This was especially true in the community where Grandpa Colby lived, where being able bodied was essential to earning a livelihood. But Grandpa Colby simply found a way, as many people do, of living well without the benefit of the full body he was given at birth. He finished school and became a successful banker and family man. He was at peace. He was content, regardless of circumstance.

"Stuffocation"

Most of us have a vision of what we think is absolutely necessary for us to be happy. As we have noted, there is a measure of truth in those beliefs. But the greater truth is that we can learn to live happily even if we are denied things we consider essential.

Just as our homes have expanded over time, the list of material things we deem important continues to grow longer and longer. British author and trend forecaster James Wallman tells about a formal study by UCLA anthropologists to dig into the stuff that fills American homes. The smallest home in the study measured just under a thousand square feet, yet in the home's two bedrooms and the living room alone, researchers found 2,260 items. They counted only items out in the open, nothing hidden in drawers or cupboards. Among all the homes in their study they found on average:

- 39 pairs of shoes
- 90 DVDS or videos
- 139 toys

- 212 CDs
- 438 books and magazines

Wallman says of the homes studied, "Nine out of 10 had so many things that they kept household stuff in the garage. Three quarters of them had so much stuff in there, there was no room left for cars." The UCLA anthropologists call this a "clutter crisis." Wallman calls it "stuffocation," which he defines as "suffocating under too much stuff." He adds that the overgrowth of clutter is not solely an American phenomenon: the average British woman "buys 59 items of clothing each year, she has twice as many things in her wardrobe today as she did in 1980, and she has 22 things in there she has never worn."[1]

We think it's safe to assert that people—both women and men—in any developed society would recognize themselves in these concrete examples of "longing for more." Without a conscious change of direction, this is where we live. But how can we move past our insatiable cravings to a genuine contentment?

How can we move past our insatiable cravings to a genuine contentment?

Let's look at some attitudes and practices that can help us affirm and act on some of the self-assessment statements on the Contentment Continuum.

"I am confident in God's love for me."

We have already encouraged a practice that helps in growing our sense of God's love—participating in the life of the church, where we regularly hear the Good News of our acceptance and destiny in Christ. We have also noted how personal prayer and Bible reading can reinforce our moment-to-moment appreciation of these foundational truths. Now is the time to reinforce those practices. In particular we want to tie our confidence in God's love to a new mindset toward money and material things and see how the Bible consistently draws that connection.

Scripture celebrates that God lovingly provides what we need *and* tells us that things will never satisfy us in any sort of ultimate way. The Bible resounds with encouragement for us to work hard to acquire what we need *and* to avoid the trap of believing that money or things will make us happy or content. It tells us to use and enjoy things *without* letting them cause us discontent.

Here are a few of many examples:

"Whoever loves money never has enough; whoever loves wealth is never satisfied with their income. This too is meaningless," says Ecclesiastes (5:10).

And then there are these words from Proverbs 1:19: "When you grab all you can get, that's what happens: the more you get, the less you are" (MSG).

Jesus talks about the same idea in terms of peace. The calm we all long for doesn't come from possessions but from him. "Peace I leave with you; my peace I give you," he says. "I do not give to you as the world gives. Do not let your hearts be troubled and do not be afraid" (John 14:27).

The apostle Paul in Philippians 4 puts forth one of the Bible's more extended teachings on worry and peace. First he says that we should trade worry in for prayer: "Do not be anxious about anything, but in every situation, by prayer and petition, with thanksgiving, present your requests to God. And the peace of God, which transcends all understanding, will guard your hearts and your minds in Christ Jesus" (verses 6-7). (We also like the way *The Message* puts it: "It's wonderful what happens when Christ displaces worry at the center of your life.")

In addition to prayer, Paul encourages us to focus our minds on things other than what worries us: "Whatever is true, whatever is noble, whatever is right, whatever is pure, whatever is lovely, whatever is admirable—if anything is excellent or praiseworthy—think about such things. Whatever you have learned or received or heard from me, or seen in me—put it into practice. And the God of peace will be with you" (Philippians 4:8-9).

Paul isn't making up wild theories. His teaching comes from his own experience riding a roller-coaster of joy and suffering, plenty and want. As a result of what he learned, he was able to say, "I have learned to be content whatever the circumstances. I know what it is to be in need, and I know what it is to have plenty. I have learned the secret of being content in any and every situation, whether well fed or hungry, whether living in plenty or in want. I can do all this through him who gives me strength" (Philippians 4:11-13).

Paul describes exactly what Brad's Grandpa Colby discovered. Peace doesn't come from outward circumstances but from an inward surrender to Christ.

"I have learned the secret of being content in any and every situation."

The fact that Scripture raises the topic of worry and peace so often suggests this is a common human struggle. But to be honest, these verses can both encourage and discourage us! Yes, we should pray. Yes, we should think about more noble things. Yes, we should be content. But how do we get there day to day? The answer lies in putting some practical tactics into action.

"Tithing—giving 10 percent—is an important part of how I manage my money."

The 2000 Social Capital Community Benchmark Survey of 30,000 American households found that those who donated to charity were 43 percent more likely than nongivers to say they were "very happy."[2] This research doesn't prove which comes first— giving or happiness—but we believe the two absolutely go together. The real-life experience of many generous people fits with the famous insight of Jesus that it is "more blessed to give than to receive" (Acts 20:35).

While the New Testament transcends the Old Testament law that commanded people to give a tithe back to God, the principle remains a common guideline for giving. Tithing means taking 10 percent of what you earn and giving it for God's work in the world. This is another "generosity discipline" we want to encourage you to consider. It's a practice for learning contentment regarding what we earn and own. Often the theme of tithing comes up in the context of giving to a local church. We want you to think of it as a yardstick for giving in general—not as a law but as an invitation and challenge.

Many people would agree that this level of generosity is a good idea. Most recognize it as a stretch. The sacrifice often seems so great, however, that the most common reaction to this proposal is, "I just don't have enough left over to give any of it away." If we haven't established a habit of proportional generosity, we look at that 10 percent figure and gulp. It seems impossible to recast our budgets to give that much. But recent research suggests there may be a way forward, and at first it may entail giving less!

The research was described in a book called *Switch: How to Change Things When Change Is Hard*, by Chip Heath and Dan Heath.[3] The Heath brothers make their living as research professors, studying how human behavior can be changed. One of their insights is called "Shrink the Change." Take housecleaning, for example. They encourage us to clean for ten minutes and then stop, considering that a success. If we tell ourselves we need to clean the whole house or unclutter the entire overstuffed garage, we might never get started. By making the goal easily attainable (who can't spend ten minutes cleaning?) we get ourselves started.

When it comes to being generous with money, if giving 10 percent feels out of reach, start with one percent more than you give right now. Aim to increase by one percent every three to six months until you reach your goal. As you connect giving to your everyday life, you will soon see that you really do have enough. Sharing not just money but time and energy will feel not just more doable but more joyful. Remember, giving from a surplus mindset is *not* linked to how much money you have; rather, it is choosing to lead with generosity in all its forms.

"I am comfortable with what I have and what I give away."

A generosity discipline that goes a long way to cultivating this even-keeled attitude is budgeting. Many people find they stop worrying about having enough when they start planning.

The writer of Proverbs puts it well: "Careful planning puts you ahead in the long run; hurry and scurry puts you further behind" (Proverbs 21:5, MSG).

People often avoid budgeting because it reveals how little money they have to do all the things they want to do and how little they have to buy all the things they want to buy. Budgeting indeed provides a reality check. But when we plan from a perspective of faith—that is, when we realize our money comes as a trust that we are called to manage for God—that changes everything. Budgeting isn't about getting what we want. It's about using our money for God and for others.

Many people find they stop worrying about having enough when they start planning.

To be sure, that includes taking care of our own needs and bills. A realistic plan makes sure those items get paid. That alone liberates us from numerous worries and leads us to feel more relaxed about what we have and what we can give. We don't have to feel guilty about spending on ourselves or fretful about giving too much to others, because we have planned for it.

There's more. Budgeting also helps us trust God. That statement might sound like a contradiction. If we really trust God to care for us, why plan? And if we plan, are we really trusting God to provide? The way this often plays out in daily life suggests that a combination of trust and planning ahead leads to an enhanced sense of security.

In our experience we have found this is one of the paradoxes that financial professionals discover time and again. Thrivent had a revelation about this while conducting focus groups. Thrivent asked participants about retirement planning—specifically, whether they thought their planning would meet their needs, and what they would do if it didn't. One set of people exhibited little if any fear in their answers. Their reasoning wasn't "I don't worry about it; the Lord will provide." Ultimately that's true, but that spiritual-sounding attitude can also be an excuse not to plan. No, the answers we heard were more along the lines of "I'll make do."

At first Thrivent thought this was yet another way to dodge wise financial planning—until they dug a little deeper. Thrivent researchers eventually discovered the "I'll make do" group had disconnected wealth from security, and circumstance from happiness.

The people in this group were ready to take care of themselves, their families, and their communities now and in the future because of their thoughtful planning. These folks would adapt their lifestyles to live within their means. Because they had planned for the future, they were able to live one day at a time. And they had determined that if things didn't work out in the future, they would simply adjust.

Healthy planning begins by making time to meet with a financial guide—someone you trust to give you honest, accurate advice and who understands your values and beliefs. Careful planning can make a difference in the well-being of people who are insecure about their future. As they plan, they likely will discover a paradox. The more they plan for their future, the more they realize they really don't control it. Yet the more they plan, the less anxious they feel, the more they can live for today, and the more generous they may become with all they have and are.

That sounds a lot like the surplus mindset, doesn't it? How much money you have never determines how easy it is for you to give it away. Now that is liberating!

"There's enough for everyone."

When you hear the phrase "There is enough for everyone," it's often followed by a request for a donation. Since by now you know we are fans of generosity, clearly we believe that folks who have more than they need should share with those who don't have enough. However, that may not be the best way to help all families build security and wealth. Rather than charity or even smart investing, risk pooling has proven to be a highly effective strategy to provide enough for everyone.

Risk pooling has proven to be a highly effective strategy to provide enough for everyone.

Adam Smith, the Scottish economist credited with establishing many principles of modern capitalism, describes risk pooling this way: "The trade of insurance gives great security to the fortunes of private people by dividing among a great many that loss which would ruin an individual, and thus make it fall light and easy upon the whole society."[4]

Fraternal Benefit Societies in America and their predecessors—Friendly Societies, Guilds, Widows and Orphan funds, the Community Chest, and similar organizations in most every culture—were created to pool risk, provide for those in need, and encourage members to "carry each other's burdens" (Galatians 6:2).

When you play Monopoly, you sometimes draw a card called "Community Chest," which instructs you to put some of your money in the communal pot in the middle of the board, not knowing who might receive it down the road. A real-life form of a "community chest" is the United Way, an organization that fund-raises on a grand scale and then supports thousands of local non-profit community organizations. This community chest idea actually goes back hundreds of years to the days of Martin Luther.

In the north of Germany, in the Mittelsachsen district in the state of Saxony, lies the town of Leisnig. Sometime in 1522 and again in 1523, Martin Luther visited Leisnig to help the community write what today is known as the Leisnig Order of Casts. It was an attempt to institutionalize the practice of generosity for the whole town.

The Order of Casts is a document outlining how the community would provide for compassionate and generous treatment of the less fortunate. A community chest was established from which funds could be distributed, with money coming from voluntary gifts, inheritances, alms, rents, and incomes.

A council of ten annually elected trustees supervised these funds. There were clear requirements for the council makeup. They had to come from four groups of citizens: two directors would come from the nobility, two from the existing city council, three from the common citizenry, and three from the rural peasantry.

The funds were stored in a strongbox secured

with four locks, each with its own unique key. Each key was kept by one of the four groups represented in the council, and all four keys were required to open the chest.

As for the guidelines for using the funds, here are a few examples. Money could be given to pastors, the church custodian, the schoolmaster, orphans, and those impoverished by circumstance, old age, or illness. Loans could be made to those out of work or who were new to the parish community. Money was used for the education and healthcare of children, and low-interest loans were given to artisans and craftsmen. Daughters of the poor would be given dowries so they could marry rather than face a lifetime of domestic servitude.

Each week the directors met to decide how to disburse funds. Records were kept of meetings and all contributions and disbursements. Three times each year, the entire parish met to review and make decisions about the fraternal agreement, and they received an annual report from the trustees.

The four-lock community chest was used from 1523 until at least 1806, according to our research. That's 283 years! Here was a town that—with the guidance of Martin Luther, a great champion of God's generous grace—devised a way to live generously as a community. Their model taught a radically new money mindset to an entire village. They proactively embraced the reality that they would always have all kinds of people among them, from those struggling to survive to others living in surplus. We can still learn from their legacy, and there are certainly other examples in the church and in the world that can teach us about intentional generosity on a scale that impacts whole communities and more.

Do we still need to pool risk, provide for "widows and orphans," and encourage "carrying one another's burdens" today? The short answer is yes, as much as ever. While government has assumed the role of providing a social safety net for the most needy, a potential recipient must normally use up all family wealth to be eligible. And while charity certainly blesses those in need and those who give, it sadly provides nowhere near enough and often serves only the most needy. Even if "widows and orphans" receive assistance, other genuinely deserving people fall through the cracks. Bearing one another's burdens through risk pooling is vital for everyone living above bare survival. It's the single best way to protect wealth and at the same time truly ensure there is enough for everyone.

We touched on this topic in chapter 4, but let's get down to details. The life events where many people should pool risk are health, disability, early death, property, long-term care, and longevity (outliving your resources). While you can't currently purchase insurance for job loss, you can self-insure by having an emergency savings amount of at least equal to the length of time you believe it would take to find a new job.

We believe that in America, too many people are without insurance. We want to urge you not to wait until it's too late. Too many postpone action until they are no longer insurable. Remember that the government extends special tax benefits to many life, health, and retirement insurance products. So these products can be both a smart choice and a wise use of your resources. Look for an insurance company that is strong and stable, since at times the promise to pay will be decades away.

Here's our underlying point. Pooling risks with others frees us to live in greater peace, because we know that others will bear our burdens as we commit to bearing theirs.

Knowing What You Want

Sometimes contentment and peace come by managing our expectations.

I (Jim) recall a video clip from some years ago telling the story of a wise young woman whose insights into *wanting* produced a beautiful result. It showed a young woman sitting in front of an older male television documentary host. She looked to be in her early thirties, blonde and soft-spoken. Her eyes and facial structure made it apparent that the young woman lived with Down syndrome.

After a few moments of preparation by the TV personality, the interview began. This woman had recently married a man who also lived with trisomy 21, another name for Down syndrome. Since marriage among Down's persons is rare, their lives become a curiosity.[5]

The interviewer wanted to know how they managed. Were they happy? How did they pay their bills? Since they couldn't drive, how did they get to work? They would never produce biological children because of their agreement to be sterilized before the wedding. They lacked the intellectual capacity to dive into conversations about politics, religion, and global warming. And the "great American dream" of home ownership seemed far beyond their reach. How could they possibly be satisfied?

Sometimes contentment and peace come by managing our expectations.

The woman paused for a moment after the barrage of inquiries about her happiness. She looked the interviewer in the eyes and said slowly and confidently, "I am happy because I always get what I want."

Dumbfounded, the interviewer went back over the litany of things the woman and her disabled spouse would never have. With incredible poise, this young woman repeated her point: "I always get what I want. But I know what to want."

The young woman explained that her happiness was rooted in realistic expectations for her life. She didn't believe she would be the next Nobel laureate or even a highly skilled white-collar worker. On the contrary, because she had settled in to her place on the planet rather well, she was able to live in contentment.

"I always get what I want. But I know what to want."

Can you say that you know what to want? Out of her wisdom and joy, this woman shared the secret to living at peace.

CHAPTER 10

LONGING FOR SUCCESS

PREACHING PROFESSOR FRED CRADDOCK relates a whimsical conversation with a greyhound that reveals much about our longing for success.

Rescued from a racetrack, the greyhound was making the most of his new home, playing with the children who now filled his days. Craddock says, "Hey, Dog, why aren't you racing anymore? Are you too old?"

The dog says, "Oh no, I'm still young."

"Well, why aren't you racing anymore? Weren't you winning races?"

"Oh yes," says the dog. "I was winning races right up until I quit."

"Then why did you quit?"

The dog says, "One of these days you'll realize what I realized. *I realized that the rabbit I was chasing wasn't real.*"[1]

Success matters—up to a point. But pursuing it above all else is like a greyhound chasing a fake rabbit. At the end of an exhausting race, we are right back where we started.

Chasing Success

The usual definitions of success revolve around money and power. Dictionary.com, for example, defines it as "the attainment of wealth, position, honors, or the like."[2] Many people in the United States and around the world believe that success of every kind is within reach. The international consulting firm Accenture recently polled 4,100 executives from thirty-three countries to better understand how professionals define success. They found that more than 70 percent of both men and women from around the world believe they can "have it all," defined as "a successful career as well as a full life outside work."[3]

We live in an age of excess. There seems to be no end to the voices telling us to accumulate possessions, property, position, and power. All of this sends a subtle but commanding message: *You need to look like this person or achieve this status or have all this stuff if you want to feel good about yourself.* At no other time in history has it been so easy to feel like a failure as you compare yourself to countless images of so-called "success."

The apostle Paul calls out the dangers of pursuing success without regard for the more important things of life. He passes down wisdom to his protégé Timothy, giving the young pastor a message to share with those in his congregation who longed for nothing more than worldly success. Paul explains the perils that await these folks. He writes, "Those who want to get rich fall into temptation and a trap and into many foolish and harmful desires that plunge people into ruin and destruction" (1 Timothy 6:9).

Paul calls out in particular the single-minded pursuit of money. He says, "The love of money is a root of all kinds of evil. Some people, eager for money, have wandered from the faith and pierced themselves with many griefs" (1 Timothy 6:10). The first part of this famous saying is frequently misquoted as "Money is *the* root of *all* evil." But the Bible distinguishes between *having* money and *buying* things on one hand and having an excessive *love* for them on the other. It is the *love of money* that is *a* root of *all kinds of evil.* Putting financial success at the center of life can cause people to invite all kinds of troubles into their lives and even to abandon their faith.

A few verses later Paul continues his urgent warning. Notice how he follows up with encouragement that sends us in a new and improved direction. He says, "Tell those rich in this world's wealth to quit being so full of themselves and so obsessed with money, which is here today and gone tomorrow. Tell them to go after God, who piles on all the riches we could ever manage—to do good, to be rich in helping others, to be extravagantly generous. If they do that, they'll build a treasury that will last, gaining life that is truly life" (1 Timothy 6:17-19, MSG). The riches God will add aren't necessarily material. They include, most notably, a relationship with him that begins now and lasts forever (see John 17:3). The steps we are to take along our winding path to heaven include doing good, helping others, and practicing extravagant generosity, all features of a new money mindset.

It is the love of money *that is* a *root of* all kinds of evil. "

Remember: all our longings—for security, for independence, for more, and for success—are at their root good, even God-given. The Bible assumes that God has made us to want to succeed, especially in the most important areas of life. Jesus appeals to this innate desire when he tells the parable of the talents. He suggests that we should admire the servants who do well in taking their master's money and multiplying it. They demonstrate strategic intent, shrewd tactics, and superior results. To each of these successful servants, the master says, "Well done, good and faithful servant!" (Matthew 25:14-30). In light of all we see in society and Scripture, it seems our challenge is to discover the right definition of success.

As we are all too aware, our legitimate longing to be successful easily gets out of hand. As the New Money Mindset Assessment shows, that lack of control manifests itself in several different ways. Let's check some of the statements from the Calling Continuum that highlight this.

Our challenge is to discover the right definition of success.

"The only way I'll ever be successful is if I win the lottery."
I (Jim) can't claim I have ever won the lottery, but years ago I felt like I came close. I was a cash-strapped student traveling from California to Colorado. I was speeding—literally—across the great state of Nevada, naively following the advice of an in-the-know classmate who told me over and over that "they never stop you for speeding in Nevada." Au contraire.

When an officer of the law flashed his lights, flipped on his siren, and pulled me over, my fine was $180. Since I had the option of paying on the spot, I gave the officer my Bank of Hawaii Visa card number, signed on the line, and drove away.

Within an hour, I saw signs of Las Vegas along the highway. I mean literal signs. Hundreds of them. CHEAP ROOMS. SATELLITE TV. SWIMMING POOL. JESUS SAVES SINNERS. HUGE LUNCH BUFFET—$5.99. That last one hooked me. I pulled into the Sands Hotel parking lot and headed in for some cheap food, still stinging from my $180 fine. I hadn't even eaten when I got the bright idea that maybe I should try to make up my loss at the one-armed bandits blinking all around me.

I took out a five-dollar bill and cashed it in for five one-dollar coins. I walked over to the dollar slots and saw a sign that read "$1 MILLION GRAND PRIZE." I hoped my luck would be better here than on the Nevada Interstate.

It was.

The second coin I dropped into the machine produced a *ding-ding-ding clink-clink-clink* sound I had never heard before as bells rang and coins dropped into the shiny chrome tray at my waist. They were one-dollar coins, fifty of them, to be exact!

I started shaking. Something came over me that felt like euphoria. At the same time, I knew I had to get out of there—fast. I allowed myself five more tries at the jackpot. After losing five one-dollar coins, I exited the casino still quivering, feeling I was striding against a mighty wind pushing me back inside.

That was my first and last experience with Las

Vegas gambling. It's exhilarating to win anything, but for some of us, winning money gets our blood rushing like nothing else. It makes us feel invincible, as though we will succeed at anything we undertake. Why? Because in this culture we have convinced ourselves that money is the easiest route to happiness. And the easiest, fastest, biggest way to acquire money is to win a jackpot or the lottery. We know this is a lie—the idea that winning the lottery is the key to happiness—but we still find ourselves fantasizing about what we would do if we could cash in the big ticket!

This gambler's mentality often plays out in more socially acceptable ways. We observe it in people who are always maneuvering to make a fast buck rather than execute plans that bring steady, sustainable growth. Entrepreneurs, business diehards, and all of us with plans to grow our money and prosper need to contemplate this wisdom from the book of James:

> Now listen, you who say, "Today or tomorrow
> we will go to this or that city, spend a year
> there, carry on business and make money."
> Why, you do not even know what will
> happen tomorrow. What is your life? You
> are a mist that appears for a little while and
> then vanishes. Instead, you ought to say, "If

> it is the Lord's will, we will live and do this
> or that." As it is, you boast in your arrogant
> schemes. All such boasting is evil.
> JAMES 4:13-16

Instead of repeatedly betting on yet another high-risk venture to grow our wealth, we can invite God to guide our steps and shape our plans. What we attain and acquire is in the end up to him. Proverbs speaks highly practical wisdom when it says, "Trust the Lord with all your heart, and don't depend on your own understanding. Remember the Lord in all you do, and he will give you success" (3:5-6, NCV).

"I would be happier if my salary went up by 25 percent."
"I can never seem to have quite enough money for myself."

Everyone has an internal craving for success. You know you have it. We all do. Yet more than ever before in history, it's easy to feel like a failure when we compare ourselves to the rich and famous. Television, the Internet, and all kinds of media make side-by-side comparison far too easy. Have you ever looked at a model in a magazine and thought, *I'm fat*? How many times each week do you see people who appear to have more materially than you and wonder, *Why them and not me?* We are bombarded by images that make us feel inferior as we attempt to be successful like "everyone" else.

Having spent the first dozen years of my career as a clinical therapist, I (Jim) have met hundreds of people wrestling with this chal-

We are bombarded by images that make us feel inferior.

lenge. More times than I can remember, clients expressed yearnings that ran along these lines:

- "I wish I could be more attractive."
- "I want to lose twenty pounds."
- "If I could just afford a little place up north."
- "I wish I could drive a better car."
- "If only I made another $10,000 a year."

The underlying question in each case was, *What do I need to do to feel successful?*

The answer seemed to be, *Just a little more.*

We probably never say out loud that to be happy we need to look like a supermodel or be a superstar professional athlete or have a millionaire's bank account. We don't necessarily dream in those extremes. Yet, as we have noted, most of us chase "more" of something. Maybe just *a little bit* more. That would surely be enough to make us happy.

Back in chapter 4 we shared the Boston College research that debunks the notion that having a little more will make us happy. Even the super-rich thought that 25 percent more income would let them feel bliss. But if we are honest, we can admit that whenever we indeed get more, we still come up empty. Real happiness comes from remaking our attitudes, practicing a surplus mindset that recognizes that we already have enough for ourselves and enough to share.

When we let a longing for success drive our lives, we lose sight of the abundant life Jesus offers and become engrossed in the never-attainable images of perfection.

Where has this happened to you? When the latest technology is released, do you camp out in front of the store to get your hands on it? Do you have a fondness for expensive clothes? Do you always buy the best power tools? What kind of automobiles captivate your attention? Are you living in a house that costs more than you can afford?

Or do you chase a different form of success? Maybe it's not so much about money. How do you seek status? To what lengths will you go to get everyone in your neighborhood to like you? How do you react when a coworker or competitor gets the recognition you wish would come to you?

People who long to "get rich" in any of these ways risk falling into a trap that plunges them to destruction.

"Having enough money is how I define whether I'm successful or not."

There is a study that points out a particular human behavior almost too bizarre to believe. This solid piece of research, called "The Last Place Aversion Paradox," was reported in *Scientific American* and later in *The Economist.*

The study demonstrates how much success matters to us, shown by how far we go to maintain our place in the world's pecking order. Subjects were given the choice of sharing two dollars with those who had less or giving it to those who had more. We assume that people would of course give to those who had less, right? And they did—except if giving to those who had less would land themselves at the bottom. Participants then consistently gave money to those who had more.

The research suggests how strongly we don't want to be seen on the bottom rung of the economic ladder. Rather than give two dollars to people who have less—enabling them to rise above our financial status and making us the new bottom—we prefer to give to those who already have more than us. We avoid being on the bottom because it represents failure.[4]

Gauging our success by how much we have is an area where we truly need to recalibrate our thinking. Anyone reading this book is probably quite wealthy by any global measure. Credit Suisse reported in 2014 that having a net worth of just $3,650 makes you richer than 50 percent of the world's population.

Owning an old car gets you there. Possessing $77,000 in assets puts you in the top 10 percent. That's not a small amount of money, but it shows that it doesn't take millions in the bank to make you fabulously wealthy compared to the rest of the world. And to rank as a member of the richest one percent of the global population takes assets of $798,000. In some places in North America and around the world, that's a paid-off two-bedroom home. Or those assets might be the result of many years of building a retirement nest egg.[5]

Having a net worth of just $3,650 makes you richer than 50 percent of the world's population.

Trade-Offs

The real problem comes down to how we define success. Do we accept the definition foisted on us by culture—or do we let God reshape what we value?

Economist Chris Farrell, editor of "Marketplace Money," a column about successful investing, says success comes down to what is important to you: "Personal finance is really about deciding how to live your life, figuring out what you value and putting your money behind your goals and beliefs. Personal finance is part of the lifelong endeavor to create a good life. Our relationship with money is an ongoing, evolving enterprise as our goals change and our ambitions shift."[6]

Quoting both the Nobel laureate economist Milton Friedman ("There's no such thing as a free lunch") and the Rolling Stones ("You can't always get what you want"), Farrell notes that life involves trade-offs.

Jesus talked about that trade-off when he spoke the words we mentioned back in chapter 2. "No one can serve two masters," he said. "Either you will hate the one and love the other, or you will be devoted to the one and despise the other. You cannot serve both God and money" (Matthew 6:24). He made the same point when he took the rich fool to task, along with anyone who "stores up things for themselves but is not rich toward God" (Luke 12:21).

No one forms a definition of success in a vacuum. In the United States, we are heirs to a culture that declares that the pursuit of happiness is a fundamental right. But there is a deeper meaning to that ideal than we probably know. "Happiness," as our Founding Fathers understood, includes a broader public good and a bent toward generosity that is lost in our modern mindset.

This truth becomes obvious if we backtrack to

the Greek philosopher Aristotle, who said that the purpose of acquiring virtue was to gain *eudaimonia.* This word can be translated as "happiness," but some would say the phrases "human flourishing" or "a well-lived life" more accurately reflect the original meaning.

A well-lived life. The Roman philosopher Marcus Tullius Cicero dedicated his book *On Duties* to his son, saying, "And what do I mean by a well-lived life, my son? I mean that you live a life that gives back to your country, gives back to your family, gives back to your fellow citizens." He also said, "Friendship improves happiness and abates misery, by the doubling of our joy and the dividing of our grief."

Almost certainly these are the ideas that America's founders, who were students of Greek and Roman literature, drew on for their own lives. It's what they were thinking when they changed John Locke's phrase about "life, liberty, and property" to "life, liberty, and the pursuit of happiness." When was the last time you thought of those goals as a beautiful pursuit of "life, liberty, and human flourishing"?

We form our definition of success not only from culture but from our family of origin.

Neither of us had a lot of money growing up. I (Jim) was raised in a family of five kids. We were incredibly close. Realizing how important education would be in our lives, my parents made sure all five of us graduated from college. We didn't have much money, but we spent a lot of time together. We did a lot of family activities like camping and weekend picnics around the Twin Cities. And we were really involved in church. We were there Sunday mornings, Sunday nights, and Wednesday nights. When I got older, I was there Thursday nights for youth group, plus usually on Saturdays. Our church family was a big part of life. And though we were aware of the differences between who had money and who did not, success wasn't defined by wealth but rather by how you lived your life. We discovered what every researcher now knows. Spending disposable income on experiences leads to increased happiness, while spending it on stuff does not.

We form our definition of success not only from culture but from our family of origin.

Looking back, parts of that life made it easy to live joyfully from a surplus mindset, knowing we had enough for ourselves and enough to share. Other parts made it natural to pursue outward success and hang tightly to what we had.

Many of us grow up with fears that make a surplus mindset difficult, and it's helpful for all of us to reflect on our experiences at home. It's helpful to set aside some time to consider how our families of origin shaped our attitudes and behaviors toward success. Here are a few memory joggers to consider:

- What did my family consider "success"? How did they define "failure"?
- Who in our world did we think had "arrived"? Whom did we look down on as strugglers?
- When I asked for things—favors, food, time, or money—as a child, what was the response? How often did I hear yes versus no?
- In what ways was my home a happy place—or not?
- What traumatic events did I or my family experience that caused us to live more carefully or fearfully rather than joyfully— for example, extended unemployment or an untimely death?
- When did I first hear words that reflected a surplus mindset—the belief that we have enough for ourselves and enough to share?
- How did I see my parents regularly serving others—or how did they stick more to themselves?
- What concrete acts of generosity—giving time, energy, or money—did I witness in my household?
- How did my family connect faith and finances, especially joyful giving?

Our answers to all of these questions contribute—consciously or unconsciously—to our definition of success. They might drive us to single-mindedly pursue outward prosperity, or they might have trained us to live for a higher purpose. We could write an entire book on this topic, but for now we simply want you to seek to understand some of the factors that shape you today. We hope this exercise will help you move even further into a present-day attitude of surplus. If these questions prompt you to deeper reflection, don't hesitate to get input from a friend, small group, pastor, or professional counselor.

Redefining Success

You maybe remember the job change that I (Brad) had prayerfully undertaken with my wife, Sue. I was motivated by a desire to travel less and be with my family more. My decision to leave the secular business world to work for a denominational church body involved not only working for a smaller organization but also *At its core, my choice was driven by a desire to redefine what success meant for me.* for a much smaller wage. At its core, my choice was driven by a desire to redefine what success meant for me.

I felt that before I took the new job, I should

reward myself with a prize for all my hard work in the business world—a brand-new car. I have loved automobiles since I was a kid, when I scraped and sacrificed—somewhat unwisely—to buy my first car. This seemed like an opportunity to give myself the ultimate gift. At my last job, everyone drove a nice car, and many people drove better ones than I did. As far as I was concerned, it was my turn.

On my first day, I proudly drove my new car into the parking lot, but before I could put it in park I knew I had made a mistake. My shimmering ride cost several times more than anything else in our lot. I walked quickly into the building, hoping no one saw what I had driven to work. I felt flush with foolishness, ashamed for having spent so much money on myself. What I thought was a good decision just a few weeks earlier suddenly turned into an embarrassment. I anticipated this car bringing me immeasurable happiness. It would signal success to myself and to others. But it did just the opposite, teaching me that our yearning for success has its downside.

I went back to the dealer and asked if they would take back my new car so I could drive off in something more reasonable. Fortunately, the vehicle I had bought was in short supply, and I had actually waited months to get it. So the dealer—for a fee, of course—took back the keys. I then bought a more modest used car.

If only I could change my heart as quickly as I can trade in a car! Of course I didn't like my new used car nearly as much. That led to swapping a string of used cars over the next months as I looked for one that filled my longing for well-engineered transportation. After several poor car decisions, I began to sense something was wrong. That led me to one of the pastors at my church, who suggested I fast from car shopping.

Most people don't have the compulsion to keep trading cars as I did. They might not need the radical redirection my pastor suggested. But with that nudge, I didn't buy a car for the next seven years.

Whatever success means to you, there is no doubt something out there that will regularly fool you into thinking that if you can acquire or attain it, you will be satisfied and therefore happy. It might be a bigger home. Or a new pair of shoes. Or a set of golf clubs. Or it might be more about power, position, status, or even fame. But God has a better definition of success. He invites each of us to live out a unique individual calling. Let's go there now.

CHAPTER 11

LIVING IN OUR CALLING

AN EXTRAORDINARY FOLLOWER OF JESUS once said, "Nowadays one sees a scrambling after riches from the lowliest station up to the highest, even among those who want to be called Christians. . . . But such behavior may well be called a life of swine. For the strongest hog at the trough pushes the others away, as though it wanted to devour everything alone."[1]

We wouldn't be shocked to hear that sentiment aimed at the "pigs" of Wall Street or the "one percenters," the world's most wealthy. But those words are nearly five hundred years old, penned by the reformer Martin Luther. When it comes to gaining a new money mindset, it seems we all live in challenging times. No matter where or when we live, we face an array of social, economic, and personal forces enticing us to pursue material success above all else.

How do we escape those pressures? How do we gain a different perspective? The Bible tells us the answer has to do with exchanging our longing for success with living in our calling—that is, following the purposes God has for each of us.

Blessed to Be a Blessing

The idea that each person has a unique calling from God begins with Abraham. The Old Testament narrative of Israel starts with Abraham's "call," a specific invitation the Lord extended to Abraham as he dwelled in the land of Ur. He was to leave his home for a new life nearly a thousand miles away (see Genesis 12:1-3). God promised that blessings would flow both to and from this man of faith. The Lord would not only provide Abraham with abundant blessings but also make him a blessing to others. God vowed, "All peoples on earth will be blessed through you" (12:3).

As children of faith, we, too, can expect a call from God. And we are all "blessed to be a blessing."

Because of God's generosity, we know what real generosity is. As a reflection of his abundant gifts, we are called to give to others on his behalf. Through his lavish provision, we have everything we need to share with others in our own meaningful ways.

While most of humanity continues to pursue success in all its forms, God points us in a different direction. The Bible goes so far as to assert that God already has a pathway mapped out for each of us. The apostle Paul writes, "We are God's masterpiece. He has created us anew in Christ Jesus, so we can do the good things he planned for us long ago" (Ephesians 2:10, NLT).

We are all "blessed to be a blessing."

There is an anecdotal story about Martin Luther in which he was approached by a man who happily announced he had recently become a Christian. Eager to serve God, he asked Luther, "What should I do now?" The man was probably expecting to hear he should abandon his old life, check into the monastery, and become a pastor or an evangelist.

"What is your work now?" Luther asked.

"I make shoes."

"Then make a good shoe," Luther replied, "and sell it at a fair price."

God's call might not come to us in a dramatic way as it did to Abraham, nor will it necessarily require uprooting ourselves to a new land. It *might* mean doing something new. Or it might entail doing the same old thing with a completely new devotion to the Lord. But God extends a call to each of us. He calls us to fulfill a variety of roles in our lives—sometimes several roles at the same time at home, at work, and at church. Living your calling means finding and fol-

Living your calling means finding and following God's unique purposes for you.

lowing God's unique purposes for you.

Let's look at the self-assessment statements on the Calling Continuum; then we'll explore some practical steps we can take to help us honor our callings.

"It is important for me to understand what God is calling me to do."

Living your unique calling starts with understanding what God wants you to do. How exactly do you obtain that kind of divine direction? An excellent place to start is by discerning your spiritual gifts. In 1 Corinthians 12:4-11, the apostle Paul outlines a sample of these God-given abilities.[2] He writes,

> There are different kinds of gifts, but the same Spirit distributes them. There are different kinds of service, but the same Lord. There are different kinds of working, but in all of them and in everyone it is the same God at work. Now to each one the manifestation of the Spirit is given for the common good. To one there is given through

the Spirit a message of wisdom, to another a
message of knowledge by means of the same
Spirit, to another faith by the same Spirit,
to another gifts of healing by that one Spirit,
to another miraculous powers, to another
prophecy, to another distinguishing between
spirits, to another speaking in different
kinds of tongues, and to still another the
interpretation of tongues. All these are
the work of one and the same Spirit, and
he distributes them to each one, just as
he determines.

Notice that there is a variety of "gifts" and "service" and "working," but the Holy Spirit empowers
them all. And "each one" receives
some manifestation of the Spirit, *We are to use the*
as he determines. Why does God *talents God has given*
give these gifts? For "the common *us to bless others.*
good" (verse 7), or as other trans-
lations put it, "so we can help each other" (NLT) or "for
the profit of all" (NKJV). *The Message* paraphrase sums
it up well: "Everyone gets in on it, everyone benefits."
    This promise of giftedness equips us for what we
call the generosity discipline of talent. We are to use
the talents God has given us to bless others.
    How you uncover your special abilities isn't a
mystery. It's a simple matter of trying them out,

volunteering for this and that until you discover where your passions and talents deliver the most benefit to others.

Some areas clearly might not be worth pursuing. For example, neither of us has a knack for painting, so we stay away from opportunities with a high likelihood that we will go home covered in paint. But we can both cook and cheerfully serve food. And we both have skills to guide entrepreneurs and others trying to better their communities.

You can find opportunities all around you to stretch yourself, and the best way to discover your giftedness is to give many things a try. The more you do, the more you can fine-tune your serving, even within the same setting. A day camp, for example, needs everything from administrators to counselors to cooks. If you discover one role doesn't fit you, it's likely another one does. When you find your groove, practice. A talent that feels comfortable can almost always be further developed.

Some people seem to have multiple gifts, showing talent at a variety of tasks. All of us need to focus our serving so we don't become overextended. Here are some points worth considering. When you are living your call,

- you and others feel restored.
- people notice and affirm your gifts.

- serving causes you to feel whole, satisfied, and rewarded.
- you feel a soul-filling sense of *I was made for this*.

Besides using those points as a gauge of your fit for a particular kind of service, you can also ask people who observe you to give you tips and honest feedback.

To guide you in your exploration, you can dig into any of many spiritual gifts inventories available online or through your church. Becoming confident in your gifts goes a long way toward helping you discern your calling. And attempting to use your talents to serve others is always an act of generosity, joyful giving in the flesh. Living out the various ways God calls you shows a surplus mindset at its best.

One Life, Many Callings

Sometimes a calling can span a lifetime. But what God has planned for us may shift, change, contract, or grow through the seasons. Brad's wife, Sue, often says she is on her fifth career. We say she has had many callings, each building on the others. We also notice she has had multiple callings at the same time.

Let's start with those many simultaneous callings. Sue is a spouse to Brad. She is the mother of their children, and even though their kids are grown and on their own, she still supports and encourages them. She also works full time as a ministry entrepreneur, helping launch an urban ministry center providing job and life skills for immigrants and others in the neighborhood. Sue lives out additional callings, like being a church member and volunteer, but you get the point.

Sue also demonstrates how one calling often builds on another. God takes the talents he puts in us to bless others and multiplies them through life experiences we acquire to make them even more effective. Sue started off wanting to be a chemist, but the realities of chemistry lab sent her in other directions. So her first vocation was in the business world as a computer programmer. She worked on big systems for investment, accounting, and human resources. As she built her skills, it became apparent she had a rare quality of being able to talk both to programmers and to end users. She also displayed leadership assets, so it wasn't long before she was heading a team doing far-reaching projects.

Trying to balance all of her callings, Sue then embarked on a second career as a stay-at-home mom, and soon enough more callings were added. As an avid reader, she enthusiastically signed on to help in a church bookstore ministry. After Brad changed careers, they landed at a large St. Louis church with a fledgling bookstore. Sue helped the bookstore take off and managed a vital part of the enterprise.

Church leadership next asked Sue to help launch a mission program for members to actively engage outside the church. Using her project management and entrepreneurial skills, she kicked off a large-scale, mainly volunteer-based program that served people in the neighborhood, city, state, and around the world.

Here's the fun part. Once that mission work was up and running, she was invited to help with an urban church plant next to the St. Louis University School of Medicine. The vision was to combine a coffeehouse and Head Start daycare to fund a campus ministry. By now Sue had an unusual variety of skills and experiences that uniquely fitted her for that ministry. Sue's path shows how we can fulfill many roles for God's glory and others' good, and how one calling leads to another.

The "generosity discipline of talent" is the practice of identifying our gifts and our calling and using them to serve generously. And when we put those gifts into practice, we find ourselves living in a surplus mindset more often than not. Not only will we be convinced we have enough for ourselves, but we will see we have enough to share. Doing what we are made for is a potent antidote to misplaced longings.

When we live our God-given callings, our desire to chase worldly success fades away. It furthermore is the key to developing vision, perseverance, and resolve, critical attributes for anyone who wants to make a difference for God's kingdom.

"I regularly take time to reflect and seek God's wisdom for my life."

Back in chapter 5 we discussed the discipline of prayer. Here we want to highlight a specific type of prayer, which I (Jim) call "quiet listening prayer." It's a time of slowing down, sitting still, and inviting God to "rub off on us" as we keep quiet before him. One verse that inspires this kind of prayer is Psalm 46:10: "Be still, and know that I am God; I will be exalted among the nations, I will be exalted in the earth."

When we live our God-given callings, our desire to chase worldly success fades away.

If we are still, we will know God better. That includes hearing more clearly what he calls us to be and to do.

Being still isn't easy. Who doesn't have a long list of things to get done? But time alone with God might give us clarity about what should remain on the list and what should go, and there are ways to ease into this prayer practice. You can begin by reading a brief section of Scripture at the start of your day and taking five to ten minutes to meditate on the words, letting them roll over you. Or you might choose an attribute of God on which to focus your attention, such as faithfulness, loving-kindness, generosity, forgiveness, or mercy. Or you can quiet yourself and just sit in God's presence. You might journal as you rest, recording what comes to mind.

Two things often happen during these times. Both can help you more faithfully live out your callings.

First, you might become more aware of how God's love and mercy permeate your whole existence. That alone can fill you with a gratitude that motivates you to go forth and love others with a similar mercy.

Second, you might get hints from God about who or where he wants you to serve next. Often the face of a friend will pop into your mind, or you will remember a forgotten task, or a new idea for serving others will surface.

Be gracious with yourself when your mind wanders to a million other things, because without a doubt it will drift. Don't attempt to jerk your attention back to prayer. Instead, just as your mind drifted away gently, let it come back gently to prayer. An ebb and flow is normal. Don't get anxious about quiet listening prayer, because that defeats the purpose. Just try to do a "good enough" job.

Quiet listening prayer takes time to develop into a regular discipline. It won't be easy the first time you try it, but over time you can train your heart and mind to be still before God and to listen well.

"My life has a clear sense of purpose."
Once we begin to determine our gifts and callings we need to reorient our lives around our new sense of purpose. If we don't focus how we spend our days, we suffer a consequence eloquently described by our friend and colleague Ed Klodt in his book *The Jonah Factor*:

> Many of us have gone into a deep sleep. Our lives have become routine, perhaps comfortably so. What few plans we've made for the future mostly involve maintaining the material and financial security we mistakenly cling to. Much like [the prophet] Jonah, we've gone below deck, holing ourselves up against God's plans or direction, and hoping we won't get noticed.
>
> We're following a script written by someone else, perhaps living out the expectations of our parents, our employers, our spouses, or our children. We've slipped unconsciously into lives of bondage to bosses, debts, lifestyles, and expectations.[3]

Maintaining clarity comes from regularly examining whether our lifestyle lines up with our gifts and values. The four most critical areas to monitor are money, time, talents, and relationships, and the two most important instruments for measuring those areas are our checkbooks and calendars.

Our checkbooks help us align our priorities with our spending. I (Brad) have a friend who performs a regular "personal cash flow audit" on himself. To make sure his giving, spending, and savings match his beliefs and rhetoric—that his walk matches his talk—he takes a six-month time period and analyzes his spending line-by-line. He maps everything against his beliefs and values, asking himself the hard question: Do they match? If not, he decides what he needs to alter over the next six months. It amazes him how quickly and easily everything gets out of alignment.

> *Maintaining clarity comes from regularly examining whether our lifestyle lines up with our gifts and values.*

Our calendars help us manage our time, talents, and relationships. A calendar doesn't just alert us to appointments and special occasions. It can also help us manage our talents and relationships. By actively scheduling volunteer commitments and time with loved ones, we make sure these priorities happen.

We know of one pastor who, naturally, believed

he was called to preach to his congregation. But he found that the church demands were unending. Individuals always wanted a slice of his time, and he felt a constant press of committee meetings and community functions. Finding time for the one thing he felt most called to do—preach a well-prepared sermon—was elusive. He made space for his calling simply by blocking out time in his calendar for sermon preparation. He marked those time slots as "appointment." When people asked if he could come to an event at one of those times, he would simply say, "I'm sorry, my calendar is booked then."

When you say you have something already on your calendar, people in our culture respect that. Instead of arguing with our pastor friend, people would say they understood. Had he told them he would be busy reading commentaries and theology books at that moment, they likely would have responded that he could do that anytime—and that they needed him at their meeting! By managing his time the pastor could be sure to fulfill his calling.

"It's not important for others to see me as successful."
Much of our longing to be successful is driven by two factors: wanting to accumulate things for ourselves and needing to look successful to others. Breaking free of those forces lets us live our calling in ways we could never foresee.

Living Your Insides Out

In the summer of 1912, a baby boy was born to a prominent central Georgia couple. The seventh of ten children, Clarence Jordan grew up with all the privileges of a well-off white youth in the highly segregated South.

Early in life, Clarence became deeply disturbed by the injustices he saw in his hometown of Talbotton. His keen sense of the economic and social inequities he witnessed inspired him to enroll at the University of Georgia and major in agriculture so he could help local sharecroppers farm more effectively. In 1933, he earned his degree and briefly returned home to find ways to serve the rural poor through improved farming techniques.

As the weeks went by, Clarence began to grow in his conviction that poverty and racial injustice were less a technical challenge than a spiritual one. So he enrolled in a doctoral program in New Testament studies in Louisville, Kentucky. By the spring of 1939 he had a PhD in Greek in hand and was well prepared for a life in academia.

Rather than hide away in the ivory tower of teaching or busy himself in the tasks of pastoring a local church, Clarence, with his new wife, moved back to Georgia. Along with another couple, he and Florence founded Koinonia Farm.

The families set up a 440-acre farm near Americus,

Georgia, convinced that the message of the Bible was incompatible with the segregation and racial tension so prevalent in 1940s America. At Koinonia Farm, white and black Americans would pool their financial, spiritual, intellectual, and physical resources to loosen the grip of poverty, working together across racial divides. Early participant Helen Lewis described her experience:

> I was a freshman at a small women's college in Georgia in 1941. One day Clarence Jordan spoke. During that hour, I experienced the greatest learning experience of my life. It was a true conversion experience. All the contradictions of being Southern, Christian, white, educated, and a woman confronted me. I was spellbound and fascinated, but my mind was on fire. For the first time it all made sense, and the message and mission for a Christian in the South was clear. I could never again be so complacent, or sit still, or be quiet in the face of oppression or injustice.[4]

A conscious choice to let go of the American dream was essential to Clarence's passion. He not only modeled that willingness but encouraged it in others. Clarence was once speaking to a pastor who was moaning that he couldn't get his deacons to give any more money for the janitor's salary. Clarence asked, "How many children does your janitor have?"

"Eight," the minister replied.

"And how many do you have?"

"Four."

"Do you make more money than the janitor?"

"Yes."

"I can solve your problem. You swap salaries with the janitor."

Former Fuller Theological Seminary professor William Pannell described what drove Clarence to this uncompromising pursuit of his calling:

> Clarence's life was shaped by the Scriptures.
> . . . Clarence wrapped the Word in the overall
> of a southern preacher and taught us about
> another kind of Bible translator—the kind
> that can get a man shot at and lynched in
> a hundred ways. I shall be forever grateful
> that God led me to Clarence Jordan. From
> him I learned something about Christian
> integrity—living your insides out.[5]

Clarence Jordan couldn't have given himself to the nearly impossible task of racial integration without having been moved and inspired by God's generosity as revealed in Scripture. Instead of using his extraordinary education and gifts for his own gain, he expended everything for the good of others.

This story moves us because it embodies so much of what we both care about in our lives: having authentic faith, strengthening Christian communities where we live, being wise with our money and generous with our lives. We know these changes happen only by God's grace and power in spite of the stingy natures we both have.

Instead of using his extraordinary education and gifts for his own gain, Clarence Jordan expended everything for the good of others.

Clarence Jordan passed away in 1969, too soon to witness what would become his biggest legacy. Listen to what happens next.

The Generous Calling

In 1965, young Millard Fuller had achieved his dream of getting rich. At just twenty-nine years old, he and his wife, Linda, had all the trappings of wealth. Cars, boats, houses, lake homes, and club memberships marked their opulent lives. But something went wrong with the dream.

Linda had become disconnected from her husband and ultimately had an affair, leading to a crisis in their marriage. Millard had long before disconnected from her and many others because he worked day and night to earn the money that was for him the singular sign of success.

The couple slowly began to realize that their calling was not to acquire more and more but to give themselves away, especially to the poor. In a state of desperation, Linda and Millard Fuller decided to give their wealth away and begin to follow Jesus in a radical new direction. Along the way, they made an appointment to spend an afternoon with Clarence Jordan at Koinonia Farm. They wanted to see first-hand his experiment in interdependent living, serving the poor, and breaking down racial barriers.

The Fullers' afternoon visit became a monthlong stay. The monthlong stay led to a meeting in a converted chicken coop at which a dream was born— to build housing for people who couldn't otherwise afford an adequate place to live. That dream grew into what is now known as Habitat for Humanity, which is on a path to build a million houses a year. The unselfish choices of Clarence and Florence Jordan, Millard and Linda Fuller, and many others, became a movement that brings together the needy and volunteers, recipients and givers, to create safe, affordable housing that changes lives. As Fuller once said, "I see life as both a gift and a responsibility. My responsibility is to use what God has given me to help his people in need."

How ready are you to discover and live out your

own calling? Where do you sense God giving even deeper purpose to your days? Responding to God's call is one of the most exciting and transformative parts of following Jesus. And when we all hear and heed our individual callings, we can come together to accomplish amazing things. We can even change the world! Let's see now how we can make that seemingly impossible dream a reality.

CHAPTER 12

CHANGE THE WORLD

Jesus had arrived in Jerusalem for a festival—a holy holiday—when he walked by a passage known as the Sheep Gate. He came to a pool called Bethesda, a name rooted in two Hebrew words, *beit* ("home of") and *hesed* ("grace").[1] People believed that when the water was stirred up, the first one into the pool would be cured of any illness.

At this "home of grace" Jesus found a man who had lingered by the waters for almost a lifetime. One of a crowd of people suffering there with all kinds of infirmities, he had lain crumpled on his mat for thirty-eight years, constantly watching for the pool to stir, always losing in the rush to be first into the water and to be liberated from his afflictions.

We know more about this encounter than about many in the Bible. This pool had five covered colonnades, it had a name, and we know right where it was. And we are told precisely how long this man had waited for an invisible, immeasurable expression of God's generosity.

Jesus chooses the man to receive an extraordinary gift, but what he does next we would never do. The Lord asks this man if he truly wants the healing he offers. Something in the scene must have made Jesus think the man had to be asked. Despite his lifetime of waiting, was he actually ready to receive God's generosity?

From all we know, the pool of Bethesda was beautiful, with covered alcoves to block the scorching sun, presumably clean water to quench one's thirst, and a community of friends who continually gathered there. Maybe this man wasn't sure the gift would improve his life. Maybe the paralytic existence this man knew was preferable to the life he had never known or had long forgotten as an able-bodied person. Maybe he was so at home with his situation that he couldn't envision the impact of God's grace.

So Jesus asks the man, "Do you want to get well?" The man's reply suggests he does, adding that none of his companions have ever eased him into the stirring waters.

Then Jesus makes the pool a true home of grace, displaying the generosity that others could not or would not offer. He tells the man, "Get up! Pick up your mat and walk." And at once, without even dipping a toe in the pool, the paralyzed man receives the miraculous gift of healing.

Accepting the Gift

Throughout this book we have written about a different kind of healing, a breaking free from the unease, tension, bondage, discouragement, dissatisfaction, even boredom that are consumerism's debilitating effects. We hope we have shown how our finances are deeply connected to the abundant life Jesus came to bring. We have explained that no matter where they are on the socioeconomic ladder, virtually everyone can thrive right now—personally, as a family, and as an active part of a community. We have told how *What happens next* the ripples of a healthy relation- *is up to you.* ship with money spread outward as you embrace the idea that you have enough for yourself and enough to share. But at this moment, what happens next is up to you.

Do you want to be made whole? Do you truly long

for the health described in this book? Maybe the calm waters of materialism seem too pleasant to abandon. Maybe the sun-blocking shade of keeping everything for self feels more sensible than giving ourselves away in generous acts of love.

If we want our lives to be transformed, we have to choose to accept the gift. Recall the words of Proverbs: *We live generously today.* "The world of the generous gets larger and larger; the world of the stingy gets smaller and smaller" (11:24, MSG). In the deepest part of our souls, we both want our worlds to get larger and larger with family, friends, and new acquaintances all telling stories of God's healing and liberation. But sometimes we prefer to stick around the familiar surroundings of material things and bank balances that give us security. Some days it's easier to stay with what we know, even when it has us immobilized.

God comes to us with a gift. Will we receive it with open hearts and minds? Or will we deflect his generosity with a less-than-enthusiastic response?

In accepting God's generosity, we are changed. We also become "homes of grace" to a world that desperately needs fixing. Think with us about five areas of transformation that can grow from a heart set free:

- **We act now.** By embracing the truth that God supplies all our needs, we don't have to wait until "someday when I have enough" to start acting generously. And by leading with openheartedness of time, energy, and money, we can transform the nature of our relationships, moving from a survival or struggling mindset to a surplus mindset.

Tradition held that the waters of Bethesda healed only the first person to enter after the waters stirred. This must have created a community of scarcity where a paralyzed man never found help to ease him into the pool. Choosing generosity breaks that cycle now.

- **We can get up.** The new money mindset lets us leave bondage behind and releases us to live our callings. People who never know the joy of fulfilling God's unique purposes for their lives can be depressed, ineffective, and often hopeless. People who instead embrace their calling can change the world by sharing the gifts God puts within them. Whether your talent is making beautiful furniture, creating a home that welcomes *We walk in our calling.* strangers, managing a work team, or feeding the hungry—finding and pursuing God's calling will give you confidence to step up and serve in ways you never thought possible.

- **We find new waters.** Just like the man healed by Jesus, when we receive God's generosity, our world immediately gets bigger. That man went from staking out a few square feet to strolling around God's holy city and beyond. Healing transported him from a world that extended only as far as he could see to a new life as expansive as his feet could carry him.

With Christ's transforming power, we too get a brand-new perspective. Our sphere of influence grows rapidly as we notice a community of creatures needing God's healing. We start living generously by reaching beyond our immediate circle of family and friends. Building a house, feeding the hungry, or caring for a home-bound elder are all ways to find new waters when Jesus touches us with his generosity.

- **We tell others.** We love only because God first loved us. As creatures who have experienced God's grace in the Cross of Christ, our response is like

We enjoy a larger world.

that of the man at the Bethesda pool. We can't help but tell others about the gift. John 5:9-15 shows the healed man telling the religious leaders not once but twice about the man who transformed him. He was so moved by his healing that after learning Jesus' name, he returned to the Pharisees. Generosity is contagious, as research demonstrates.[2] By sharing God's healing in our lives, we can start a movement that can change the world.

- **We finish the race whole.** The paralytic had spent decades as an invalid. Even if he had been disabled since he was a young boy, he was probably near the *We start a movement.* end of his life when Jesus healed him. Most first-century people of Israel wouldn't survive much past forty. Jesus gave this man time to create a legacy of spreading the news wherever he went about his transforming encounter with God.

I (Jim) learned as a clinical therapist years ago that many of us have been scarred by life. We bear burdens seen and unseen, and even the most "perfect" families have their secrets. But Jesus' healing is never too late. Whatever your story, however you have been wounded, saying yes to the great physician means you finish strong. Whether your legacy is how many nails you pound in homes for the homeless or how many hours you spend with a child in need, you can build a legacy starting today. It's never too late.

Real Change

The personal transformation of a new money mindset happens as we move from

longing for security to living in freedom;
longing for independence to living in community;

longing for more to living in contentment;
longing for success to living in our calling.

Growth in each of these areas helps us more consistently live in a surplus mindset, which in turn determines our readiness to share all that we have and are—including our time, energy, and money.

By now it's probably relatively easy for you to envision concrete ways your generosity can alter the landscape right around you. Maybe you can imagine your impact on an elderly neighbor, on a needy school, or on families suffering hunger, whether in plain view in urban cores or hidden in suburbs and small towns and farms.

We want to encourage you now to think even bigger and broader. Why would a business leader and psychologist encourage people to live generously? Because we love seeing transformation on an individual scale. We also truly believe that joyful generosity can change the world.

Let us give you a few practical examples to show the power of small changes in behavior that could have worldwide impact. We're going to talk simple dollars and cents about problems that seem overwhelming and intractable. But they are not.

Global Development

A change in generosity would create an enormous global economic lift for the people Jesus called "the least of these" (Matthew 25:40). That might seem obvious, but what is surprising is how little it would take. In 2013, individuals gave $240 billion to charities in the United States.[3] But the next fact is staggering: "If every household in American [sic] gave up $5 a day of 'frivolous consumption' to philanthropy . . . it would double household giving overnight and probably top $500 billion in charitable giving."[4]

That additional giving equates to another $260 billion—or more than *eight times* the entire United States nonmilitary foreign aid budget.[5] It's enough money in just one year to nearly fill the extreme poverty gap. Trend spotter Amanda Scherker puts this in terms we can understand. She reports that

- $6 billion would prevent four million malaria deaths.
- $13 billion would provide every mother and newborn in the developing world with maternal and prenatal care.
- $26 billion would give a basic education to every child in the world.
- $44 billion would totally end world hunger.
- $190 billion would provide clean water and effective sanitation to half the population lacking those basics.[6]

Put simply, a little more generosity would go a long way.

Churches

Not long ago I (Brad) was sitting with a tour group in the amphitheater in Ephesus. We were retracing the

A little more generosity would go a long way.

footsteps of the apostle Paul, and our teacher, Dr. Michael Wise of the University of Northwestern, was laying out the history of the city and insights into ancient life. He moved to thoughts about the apostles Paul and John; Jesus' mother, Mary; and the city of Ephesus. Then he asked a question I haven't been able to shake: How did a handful of Christians transform one of the leading cities of pagan Roman worship into one of the largest and most important concentrations of Christian disciples?

The conclusion? It was sacrificial love demonstrated during times of trial and disease. The practical generosity of Christians toward the community—frequently risking their lives to help those in need—changed the city.

Consider how Christian action today compares with that all-in attitude. Some modern facts:

- In 2005, United States Christians (counting only members of churches) earned well over two trillion dollars, more than the total gross domestic product (GDP) of all but the six wealthiest nations.[7]

- Most Christians still feel they are just getting by, categorizing themselves as surviving, struggling, or stable in their relationship with money, missing out on a secure or surplus mindset.[8]
- Most giving nevertheless is done by people of faith.[9] In 2013, $105 billion (31 percent of all giving) was to religious causes.[10]
- The level of religious giving has been flat or dropped since 2009.[11]
- In 2012, about 5 percent of Americans gave at a level of 10 percent (the traditional tithe).[12]
- According to one study, 16 percent of Christians give nothing to church or charity.[13]
- The average gift from regular church attendees is about 2 percent of income.[14]
- Giving generously is not necessarily correlated to income.[15]

What do all these statistics have to do with changing the world? They show that even a small uptick in joyful generosity would have a profound impact, particularly if congregations chose to use the extra income to impact their communities for good. If the average giving rose from 2 percent to 3 percent, for example, that would free up an extra $40 billion to bring about change both locally and globally.

Just as in the early days of the Christian church,

congregations that extend themselves to their communities with sacrificial love tend to thrive.

We believe the number of new Jesus followers will begin to grow once again as churches embrace joyful giving.

People

Even as we contemplate how our generosity can create change on a global scale, we want to remember that what happens with all these dollars and cents transforms real individuals. Including you.

Did you know that the past century has witnessed more than a quadrupling of real (inflation-adjusted) per capita personal income? Yet this vast growth in income hasn't translated into more generous giving. The average percentage donated to charitable causes by United States Christians has actually dropped over this period, a remarkable decline.[16] Even with this quadrupling of standard of living, we think it's obvious that contentment has not improved.

Congregations that extend themselves to their communities with sacrificial love tend to thrive.

Stop and think for a moment about the people you most recognize as being joyfully generous. What are they like to be around? What words would you use to describe them? What impact do they have on others?

Now think of people you would describe as selfish

or stingy. How do they add to your day? What do they do for others? Between the generous person and the stingy person—who makes the world a better place?

We believe that consumerism produces a contagious selfishness. Yet wanting more and more—and actually keeping much or all of it for ourselves—hasn't made people more happy and generous. On the contrary, the more readily we *share* our time, energy, and money, the more joy we discover in life.

We want a contagion of cheerful giving because that is the kind of world we want to live in. It's where we find both challenge and fulfillment. A homeless shelter in our area uses this motto in their fundraising appeals: "You may not be able to change the world, but you could be the world to one person." We believe that's true. We also believe that if you change the world for even one individual, your own world will change!

Where Are You Going?
As we have said, what happens next is up to you. Your journey to a healthy new relationship with money that reshapes you and your world begins with this book. But it lasts a lifetime. We have purposely shared the triumphs and struggles of our own journeys so you could see that truth. And as you move forward, there are three crucial questions that can

propel you on your way—questions I (Jim) was once asked by a friend.

I had finally arrived in West Africa after my long trip. I survived my first night sleeping in a mud hut in that remote Cameroonian village. The next morning I did what I always did. I set out running.

While in graduate school I had come to love the exhilaration of feeling my feet glide across the ground and push me forward mile after mile, and running had become an ingrained habit. So I laced up my running shoes, stepped out of my hut into a heavy rain, and began running through the village. Every step caused a splash of red mud, and soon I was soaked. Not more than seventy-five feet from my start, my new friend Emmanuel appeared alongside me.

The rain pelting the surrounding jungle canopy was deafening, and Emmanuel shouted at me to be heard. "Why are you running, Brother James?" I tried to explain, but he couldn't understand.

Still he continued to run beside me. He shouted a second question: "Brother James, where are you going?" I told him I didn't know. In fact I wasn't going anywhere. I was just running.

Finally, breathing hard and with some frustration in his voice, my friend said to me, "Brother James, can I go with you?"

I later discovered that several things concerned my friend as I ran through the village and looped its perimeter. "Brother James," he explained, "do you not know we have lions and a jaguar at the edge of our village? Do you not know they will kill you and eat you?"

Well, no, after just one night in town, I didn't know that!

"Brother James, we do not run in my village unless there is terrible news or we have stolen something and are trying to run away. Have you stolen something, Brother James?"

Well, no, I hadn't!

That morning as I laced up my shoes and stepped out of my hut, running had seemed so simple. But there was still so much to learn.

"Why Are You Running?"

As you take your own next steps toward a new money mindset, you can ask yourself Emmanuel's three questions.

The first is this: Why are you running? What causes you to get out of bed every day? Is it your family, your friends, your faith, your finances, your fitness, your fun, your fame—or what?

In their book *What Really Works,* Paul Batz and Tim Schmidt discuss seven ways to bring satisfaction to your life.[17] They believe that when we focus on faith, family, finances, fitness, friends, fun, and the future we can discover what really makes us run.

To be sure, many people run because they are driven by money and the pursuit of more. But it's not just money that has an unhealthy grip on us. Any of the seven things mentioned in *What Really Works* can control us if we fail to keep them in proper perspective. As many have noted, the things that have your attention control your life. In short, if any of these seven areas are grabbing your mind, heart, or body, you won't be able to handle them wisely.

We have pointed out that Jesus encourages us to be carefree, like a lily in the field or a bird in the air, trusting God to care for us (see Matthew 6:25-34). Is he telling us to shirk our responsibilities in these seven important areas? Absolutely not. Is he telling us not to plan? Never. He's just saying that in the midst of our sensible planning, we don't have to become slaves to anxiety. We don't have to run because we are worried. We can run with exuberance, knowing that no matter what happens to us, we are in the hands of a loving heavenly Father. We run because we realize that's our mission. It's what God has called us to do, and it's what will bring us the greatest delight.

"Where Are You Going?"

When we ask, "Where are you going?" we're saying, "Do you have a destination in mind?" In his book *Do Less, Be More*, John Busacker says, "Each of us has a great, unfinished life story. Your own narrative weaves together the story of *past* life-shaping events, vital *current* experiences, and inspiring dreams about the *future*."[18]

What future are you running toward? What specific goals do you want to reach in giving your time, energy, and money? Do you want to volunteer as a tutor for ten hours a week? How about going to school to get training in a talent so you can better serve others? Where should you detach from possessions that separate you from friends, from your goals, from God? How could you eventually give a tenth of your income—or even go beyond that?

We suggest you get as specific as possible in envisioning where you think God is leading you. Let's say you have decided your next goal is to provide adequately for your family. That's a worthy aim. But what does it mean to be a "good provider"? How will you know when you have arrived at a place where "good" is "good enough"? How large a salary, how much insurance, and what size house will suffice?

Looking back at the 5Ss we introduced in chapter 2, how would you describe your relationship with money? Are you struggling? Stable? Living in surplus? Where do you want to be? Where do you need to be in order to live generously and free from fear? Wherever you are today, we want to encourage you that indeed you can move toward a place where you have enough and you are prepared financially and mentally to share with others!

If you don't get clarity and commit to specific goals, you could spend your entire life thinking you have to provide more and more, and you will find yourself on a treadmill that never stops. Keep in mind that Boston College study on the super-rich. It really didn't matter how many tens of millions they had. They always felt they needed another 25 percent in order to feel secure. Decide for yourself how much is enough, set your goals, and make a strong plan to get there.

"Can I Go with You?"

The final question Emmanuel asked on that rainy morning was this: "Can I go with you?" His open-hearted willingness to join in made all the difference in reducing the likelihood that something unfortunate would happen to an unsuspecting jogger.

This question offers two dimensions for us to ponder.

The first is the vertical. One of the most poignant things about Jim's story is the meaning of his Cameroonian friend's name. "Emmanuel" means "God with us."

Wherever you run, God runs with you. In fact, God never has to inquire whether he can come along. He's always there. But he may ask, "Are you going to let me help you as I go with you?" As we have often noted, this journey isn't easy, and at times it seems impossible. But as Jesus once explained, "With God all things are possible" (Matthew 19:26). As we acknowledge his presence with us on the generosity journey, we avail ourselves of his strength and wisdom.

The second dimension of this question is horizontal, and it might be rephrased as "Who among your friends and family will go with you?" We have encouraged you to become a part of a church and even a small group. We have pointed you to get counsel from a mentor, friend, or trusted adviser. Here we reiterate how crucial it is to take this journey with others. It's next to impossible to travel this path alone, and the encouragement of friends will lead you forward.

Your New Money Mindset

As we conclude this book, we encourage you to ask yourself these three questions not just once but from time to time. Why are you running? Where are you going? Who will run with you? We trust that you will enjoy this adventure as you continue to develop a new money mindset. We are convinced that as you do, you can change the world—because our Lord, Emmanuel, runs with you.

Discussion Questions

CHAPTER 1 OUR MONEY PROBLEM

1. In your own words, what is a "money relationship"?

2. Draw a picture of your relationship with money. What are your biggest money struggles?

3. Is consumerism good—or bad? How do you see consumerism impacting your thoughts, feelings, and actions?

4. How do faith and finances go together—or not— in your everyday habits and long-term goals?

CHAPTER 2 A NEW MONEY MINDSET

1. What is a "healthy money relationship"?

2. What is a "surplus" mindset? What is your current money mindset?

3. What unhealthy money habits have you attempted to break in the past? In what ways did you succeed or fall short of your goals?

4. Why is it necessary to "start with the heart" in dealing with money issues?

5. When have you chosen to "give first" and experienced a healthier relationship with money? When have you done the opposite?

6. How does grace fuel generosity?

CHAPTER 3 READY

1. What circumstances in your own life make it a struggle to "give first"?

2. What does it mean to "add more good stuff"? Why do that? What concrete steps can you take to accomplish that?

3. What did you learn about yourself through the Money Mindset Assessment?

4. Are there areas where you already have a healthy money mindset? What are your growth points?

CHAPTER 4 LONGING FOR SECURITY

1. What steps are you taking to ensure your own financial security?

2. Agree or disagree: The size of our savings doesn't necessarily bring the security we long for.

3. How do your money habits reflect a healthy and normal drive for security?

4. What evidence do you see in your life of a scarcity mentality?

CHAPTER 5 LIVING IN FREEDOM

1. Agree or disagree: The promises of God decrease my fears about money.

2. Do you believe that God will meet your needs— or do you believe that you must fend for yourself in this world? Explain.

3. What was the most unwise life decision you ever made? How was God part of that decision— or not? How did including or excluding God impact the outcome?

4. How are you investing in a "rich relationship with God"? What benefits do you hope to gain?

CHAPTER 6 LONGING FOR INDEPENDENCE

1. Are you more prone to seek independence—or interdependence? How do you strike a balance?

2. What financial responsibilities must you assume to be a fully functioning adult? Where must you rely on others?

3. How have you seen affluence diminish connections between people?

4. When have you seen generosity build community?

CHAPTER 7 LIVING IN COMMUNITY

1. God designed us for community. What difference does that fact make in your everyday life?

2. Who are you allowing into your life to help you develop a new money mindset?

3. Agree or disagree: "The best way to gather is to scatter."

4. What concrete steps will you take to give away time, money, and energy in order to increase your connections with others?

CHAPTER 8 LONGING FOR MORE

1. What signs of a "longing for more" do you see in your life?

2. Agree or disagree: Having more—acquiring all the things and experiences money can buy—doesn't make us any happier.

3. How do you distinguish between a want and a need?

4. When has wanting more gotten you in over your head financially or strained your relationships? How were you successful in addressing that—or not?

CHAPTER 9 LIVING IN CONTENTMENT

1. When have you lacked something you considered necessary for your happiness?

2. To what extent are you "stuffocating"—suffocating under too much stuff?

3. Why is contentment a worthy goal—or not?

4. How can you move from insatiable cravings to genuine contentment?

CHAPTER 10 LONGING FOR SUCCESS

1. Whom do you know who chases excess? What results do you observe?

2. How do you define success? How prominent is money in your definition?

3. How has your family of origin shaped your definition of success? Do you find yourself conforming to that mold—or trying to live by a different definition?

4. Agree or disagree: Real happiness comes from practicing a surplus mindset—believing that we

already have enough for ourselves and enough to share.

CHAPTER 11 LIVING IN OUR CALLING

1. What does it mean that you are "blessed to be a blessing"?

2. What do you consider your unique "calling" from God?

3. How would living your unique calling change your long-term goals and daily choices?

4. What practices do you employ to regularly make sure your lifestyle lines up with your gifts and values?

CHAPTER 12 CHANGE THE WORLD

1. How has your money mindset changed since you began this book?

2. Is the idea of changing the world idealistic— or realistic? Explain.

3. What changes are you most passionate about helping bring about in the world?

4. Answer the three questions posed at the end of the book: Why are you running? Where are you going? Who will run with you?

Acknowledgments

From Brad, with heartfelt thanks . . .

To our Thrivent team—especially Randy Boushek, Knut Olson, Terry Rasmussen, Jim Thomsen, and Marie Uhrich—for their unwavering support and encouragement of this project from its earliest stages and for being faithful partners in Christ as we labor together in the mission and ministry of Thrivent.

To my family: my wife and life partner, Sue, as we have learned on the journey together; my kids, Matt and Melissa, who I'm so proud of because they live generously now; and our parents, sisters, and brothers, who love and support us.

To my godly brothers John, Kurt, and Paul, who have been there to encourage and keep me on the right path for more than forty years.

To our friends with whom we adventure through life together—Pete, Joe, Karen, William, Lori, Tim, Jeanette, Jim, Karen, Paul, Jody, Kurt, Liz, John, and Becky—for making this life a little taste of heaven.

To the church communities, many small groups,

the church leaders, and faithful friends too many to name, as they have made me a disciple of Jesus, still learning to be connected and bear fruit.

From Jim, with a heart of gratitude, I say thank you to . . .

Brad Hewitt, for inviting me into this process of sharing our passion for and struggles with generosity and faith. Your passion for Jesus, blended with your extraordinary mind, has helped open the doors of generosity for so many people.

My mentors: Dr. Donald Hall, for teaching me what it means to be a psychologist in a hurting world that needs Christ; President Emeritus Robert Holst (Concordia University, St. Paul, MN), for showing me that senior leadership, brilliant scholarship, and humility travel nicely together; retired Thrivent CEO John Gilbert, for modeling grace in the context of courageous change, both personally and professionally.

My professors at Fuller Theological Seminary and Graduate School of Psychology, for teaching me how academic rigor, Christian scholarship, and personal faith in Jesus can come together in the exciting dialog of life.

My parents, Vernon and Beverly, who after sixty years of marriage are still modeling what a Christ-centered family looks like. Thanks, Mom and Dad!

My family, Vanya, Mira, Asha, Cora, Vincent,

Jennifer, John, Joel, and Jeana. Thank you for your support across the years.

Peter, Vern, and Tom (the Guitar Stable), for faithful friendship and giving me a place to volunteer each week for more than twenty years.

Peter Bolstorff, for sharing your insights from an author's perspective.

Joel, Wayne, Jim, and Chuck (the Borderline Serious Book Club), for abiding friendship and your attempts to make me literate for the past fifteen years.

My faithful friend of fifty years, the Rev. Chips C. Paulson, the most Christlike person I know.

My friend Joel Jensen, for exhibiting joyful generosity each and every day.

Doria Camaraza, for teaching me to lead with integrity, passion, and excellence, and that hard work never goes out of style.

But especially to my daughters, Mira Elise and Asha Amari. From you I have learned laughter, joy, patience, pride, wisdom, and wonder. You each are true and amazing miracles that God placed in my life through the gift of adoption. I am so proud to be your dad, and it is to both of you I dedicate my work on this book.

From both Brad and Jim, thank you . . .

To Laura Hunter, Ed Klodt, Mark Galli, and Kevin Johnson, who all brought their unique skillsets to the project while encouraging and inspiring us to see the project through to the finish.

To the research team at Thrivent, who helped us to uncover the truth of a new money mindset.

To the team at Tyndale, for believing the message of our book was one that needed to be heard.

Notes

CHAPTER 1 OUR MONEY PROBLEM

1. Jon Alexander, "Viewpoint: How the Consumer Dream Went Wrong," *BBC News Magazine*, October 29, 2014, http://www.bbc.com/news/magazine-29786733.
2. The results of this study were reported in Graeme Wood, "Secret Fears of the Super-Rich," *Atlantic*, April 2011, http://www.theatlantic.com/magazine/archive/2011/04 /secret-fears-of-the-super-rich/308419/1/.

CHAPTER 2 A NEW MONEY MINDSET

1. The Social Metric Research and 5S Research was conducted by Thrivent's research team (Jessica Greenstein, senior research analyst), Doblin, and GfK US in a series of seven studies from 2011 to 2014. The sample group included 50,000 US Christians.
2. Ibid. While how much money we have can affect our money mindset, the amount is not as significant as what we do with what we have. Thrivent research looked at different income levels and evaluated behavior with money. The behavior that was assessed was threefold: spending no more than 40% of income on house and car; having emergency savings of at least $2,000; and either having credit cards and not using them, or using them but paying them off each month. The research indicated that people making $30,000 a year who demonstrated all three of these behaviors were much likelier to live in a surplus mindset than those who were making $100,000 per year and not following any of those three behavior guidelines with money.

CHAPTER 3 READY

1. We used two statistical procedures—multiple regression analysis and factor analysis—to narrow an original list of 300 assessment statements to the 48 best questions to help you gauge your money mindset. It's a complex process to design meaningful statements.

The design and testing of each item was carefully conducted by a group of Thrivent researchers led by Gil Young. We also sought advice from Dr. Daniel Ariely and his team at Duke University, who brought his renowned expertise on the relationship between choice and money.

2. Cara Buckley, "Man Is Rescued by Stranger on Subway Tracks," *New York Times*, January 3, 2007, http://www.nytimes.com/2007 /01/03/nyregion/03life.html; and "I Need a Hero," *Radio Lab*, http://www.radiolab.org/2010/dec/14/i-need-a-hero.

CHAPTER 4 LONGING FOR SECURITY

1. Pew Research Center, "Living to 120 and Beyond: Americans' Views on Aging, Medical Advances and Radical Life Extension," August 6, 2013, http://www.pewforum.org/2013/08/06/living-to -120-and-beyond-americans-views-on-aging-medical-advances -and-radical-life-extension/.

2. Ronald A. Berk and Joy Nanda, "A Randomized Trial of Humor Effects on Test Anxiety and Test Performance," *Humor— International Journal of Humor Research* 19, no. 4 (October 2006): 425–454, doi: 10.1515/HUMOR.2006.021.

3. Graeme Wood, "Secret Fears of the Super-Rich," *Atlantic*, April 2011, http://www.theatlantic.com/magazine /archive/2011/04/secret-fears-of-the-super-rich/308419/1/.

4. Robert Kenny, interview by Amy Novotney, "Money Can't Buy Happiness," *Monitor on Psychology* 43, no. 7 (July/August 2012): 27.

5. Melinda Wenner Moyer, "Twelve Ways to Keep You and Your Family Healthy," *Parade*, October 13, 2013, 9–10. See also "Doing Good Is Good for You: Volunteer Adolescents Enjoy Healthier Hearts," *A Place of Mind*, University of British Columbia, February 25, 2013, http://www.news.ubc.ca/2013/02/25 /doing-good-is-good-for-you-volunteer-adolescents-enjoy -healthier-hearts/.

6. "The Four-Letter Word in Advertising: Fear," *Ai* (blog), January 27, 2010, http://insite.artinstitutes.edu/the-fourletter -word-in-advertising-fear-20072.aspx.

CHAPTER 5 LIVING IN FREEDOM

1. Some of our favorites include *Contemplative Prayer* by Thomas Merton, *Prayer: Finding the Heart's True Home* by Richard Foster,

Letters to Malcolm: Chiefly on Prayer by C. S. Lewis, and *Living the Lord's Prayer* by David Tams.

CHAPTER 6 LONGING FOR INDEPENDENCE

1. Christine Pembleton, "Signs That You're Too Independent for a Relationship," Examiner.com, October 27, 2010, http://www.examiner.com/article/signs-that-you-re-too-independent-for-a-relationship.
2. Bill Ward, "Possessed by Money," *Minneapolis Star Tribune*, August 29, 2012, http://www.startribune.com/lifestyle/167858195.html.

CHAPTER 7 LIVING IN COMMUNITY

1. Boston Consulting Group, "The New Politics of the Internet: Everything Is Connected," *Economist*, January 5, 2013, http://www.economist.com/news/briefing/21569041-can-internet-activism-turn-real-political-movement-everything-connected.
2. Emily Adler, "Social Media Engagement: The Surprising Facts about How Much Time People Spend on the Major Social Networks," *Business Insider*, September 26, 2014, http://www.businessinsider.com/social-media-engagement-statistics-2013-12.
3. C. S. Lewis, "Answers to Questions on Christianity," *God in the Dock* (Grand Rapids, MI: Eerdmans, 1970), 61–62.

CHAPTER 8 LONGING FOR MORE

1. Daniel Kahneman and Angus Deaton, "High Income Improves Evaluation of Life but Not Emotional Well-Being," PNAS 107, no. 38 (August 4, 2010): 16489–16493. doi: 10.1073/pnas.1011492107.
2. Les Christie, "America's Homes Are Bigger Than Ever," *CNN Money*, June 5, 2014, http://money.cnn.com/2014/06/04/real_estate/american-home-size/.

CHAPTER 9 LIVING IN CONTENTMENT

1. James Wallman, "Viewpoint: The Hazards of Too Much Stuff," *BBC News Magazine*, January 24, 2015, http://www.bbc.com/news/magazine-30849473. James Wallman is the author of *Stuffocation: Living More with Less*.
2. Saguaro Seminar: Civic Engagement in America, Social Capital Community Benchmark Survey, The John F. Kennedy School

of Government of Harvard University, 2001. See the DARES website, http://www.donoradvising.com/press_facts.php.

3. New York: Crown Business, 2010.

4. Adam Smith, *The Wealth of Nations*, Book 1, Part 3, Article 1.

5. For another illustration of a married couple with Down syndrome, watch the documentary *Monica and David*, www.monicaanddavid.com.

CHAPTER 10 LONGING FOR SUCCESS

1. Fred Craddock, *The Cherry Log Sermons* (Louisville, KY: John Knox Press, 2001), 29–30.

2. *Dictionary.com*, s.v. "success," http://dictionary.reference.com/browse/success?s=t/.

3. "Defining Success: 2013 Global Research Results," Accenture, http://www.accenture.com/sitecollectiondocuments/pdf/accenture-iwd-2013-research-deck-022013.pdf.

4. Ilyana Kuziemko and Michael I. Norton, "The 'Last Place Aversion' Paradox," *Scientific American*, October 12, 2011, http://www.scientificamerican.com/article/occupy-wall-street-psychology/.

5. Keith Moore, "Where Do the Wealthiest 1% Live?," *BBC News Magazine*, January, 25, 2015, http://www.bbc.com/news/magazine-30949796.

6. Chris Farrell, "On Financial Opportunity Costs," *Minneapolis Star Tribune*, October 11, 2013, http://www.startribune.com/chris-farrell-on-financial-opportunity-costs/227423711/.

CHAPTER 11 LIVING IN OUR CALLING

1. *Luther's Correspondence and Other Contemporary Letters*, ed. Preserved Smith and Charles M. Jacobs (Philadelphia, 1913–18) 11, 1297f.

2. Other Bible passages where we glimpse God's wide variety of gifts are Romans 12:3-8; Ephesians 4:7, 11-12; and 1 Peter 4:10-11.

3. Ed Klodt, *The Jonah Factor: Thirteen Spiritual Steps to Finding the Job of a Lifetime* (Minneapolis: Augsburg, 2006), 74.

4. Helen Lewis, "Remembrances of Clarence: Never Again Complacent," Koinoniapartners.org, http://www.koinoniapartners.org/History/Remember.html.

5. William Pannell, "Remembrances of Clarence: Shaped by Scripture," Koinoniapartners.org, http://www.koinoniapartners.org/History/Remember.html.

CHAPTER 12 CHANGE THE WORLD

1. This account appears in John 5:1-9.
2. James H. Fowler and Nicholas A. Christakis, "Cooperative Behavior Cascades in Human Social Networks," *PNAS* 107, no. 12 (March 23, 2010): 5334–5338. doi: 10.1073/pnas.0913149107.
3. "Giving Statistics," Charity Navigator, http://www.charitynavigator.org/index.cfm?bay=content.view&cpid=42#.VVpM1PlVhBc.
4. Patrick M. Rooney, quoted in Mark Hrywna, "Americans Feeling Better, Giving More," *The NonProfit Times* Special Report /Giving USA, July 1, 2014, http://www.thenonprofittimes.com/wp-content/uploads/2014/07/7-1-14_SR_GivingUSA.pdf.
5. "Foreign Assistance Fast Facts: FY2012," USAID, https://eads.usaid.gov/gbk/data/fast_facts.cfm.
6. Amanda Scherker, "If Anybody Ever Tells You It's Too Expensive to Solve the World's Problems, Show Them This," *Huffington Post*, January 29, 2014, http://www.huffingtonpost.com/2014/01/29/solve-worlds-problems_n_4655690.html.
7. Christian Smith and Michael O. Emerson, *Passing the Plate* (New York: Oxford University Press, 2008), 12.
8. Thrivent Social Metric Research and 5S Research.
9. Alex Daniels, "Religious Americans Give More, New Study Finds," *Chronicle of Philanthropy*, November 25, 2013, https://philanthropy.com/article/Religious-Americans-Give-More/153973.
10. "Giving Statistics."
11. Ibid.
12. "American Donor Trends," Barna Group, April 12, 2013, https://www.barna.org/barna-update/culture/606-american-donor-trends#.VVter_lVhBc.
13. "Most Americans Practice Charitable Giving, Volunteerism," Gallup, December 13, 2013, http://www.gallup.com/poll/166250/americans-practice-charitable-giving-volunteerism.aspx.
14. Kent E. Fillinger, "Money Matters," *Christian Standard*, May 26, 2012, http://christianstandard.com/2012/05/money-matters/.
15. Ken Stern, "Why the Rich Don't Give to Charity," *Atlantic*, April 2013, http://www.theatlantic.com/magazine/archive/2013/04/why-the-rich-dont-give/309254/.
16. Richard J. Krejcir, "Statistical Research Comparisons to Hypotheses and Interviews," The Francis A. Schaeffer Institute of

Church Leadership Development, http://www.churchleadership
.org/apps/articles/default.asp?articleid=43900&columnid=4545.

17. Edina, MN: Beaver's Pond Press, 2011.

18. John Busacker, Do Less, Be More (Brentwood, TN: Freeman-
Smith, 2013), 43.

About the Authors

Brad Hewitt is a CEO with a unique perspective. Since 2010, Brad has served as president and CEO of Thrivent Financial, a not-for-profit Fortune 500 organization. In this role, he has made it his work to help Americans rediscover a healthy relationship with money. At the heart of this relationship is the idea that generosity and wise money management go hand in hand.

Before joining Thrivent Financial, he served a variety of organizations in various financial roles. In 1993, he was named CFO of Diversified Pharmaceutical Services, and later he became its president and CEO. He went on to serve for five years as chief administrative officer of the Lutheran Church–Missouri Synod.

Brad serves on numerous boards, including the board of regents of Concordia University in St. Paul, Minnesota; Habitat for Humanity International;

International Cooperative and Mutual Insurance Federation; and the American Council of Life Insurers. He is also cochair of the Itasca "Mind the Gap" initiative, a public/private partnership dedicated to reducing the academic-achievement and income gaps in Minnesota.

Brad holds a BS in mathematics from University of Wisconsin–River Falls and has completed the Harvard Business School's program for management development. He and his wife, Sue, have two adult children and live in Minnesota.

James Moline, PhD, believes that developing the opportunity for generosity to build God's Kingdom on earth stands as a central issue of our times. As a licensed psychologist, confidant, and advisor, Jim has built a thirty-year career consulting with global companies about providing senior leadership excellence, managing across borders, and transforming their organizations in an era of rapid change and uncertainty. As a former tenured professor, Jim is passionate about influencing lifelong learning in the communities he serves.

Jim sees his work as a calling that extends to all people in the global community of God's creation. Central to this understanding is the perspective that everything we have is a gift from God and that God calls us to live together in generous community with him. To that end, Jim's expertise extends to inspiring clients about how they can give back at the local level while helping them develop strategies and action plans that encourage philanthropy.

Along with a thirty-year commitment to teaching in the local church, Jim's personal ministry passions include Young Life International (youth), Urban Homeworks (housing), and Mobile Action Ministries (food insecurity).

In addition to being a PhD-licensed psychologist (Fuller Graduate School of Psychology), Jim also holds an MA in theology from Fuller Theological Seminary. He and his family live in Stillwater, Minnesota.

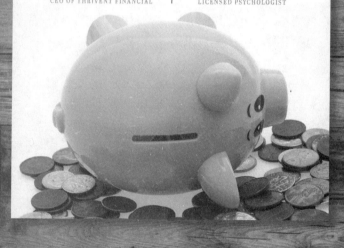

Foreword by Ron Blue, Founding Director of Kingdom Advisors

YOUR NEW MONEY MINDSET

CREATE A HEALTHY RELATIONSHIP WITH MONEY

BRAD HEWITT
CEO OF THRIVENT FINANCIAL

JAMES MOLINE
LICENSED PSYCHOLOGIST

TO LEARN MORE ABOUT
YOUR NEW MONEY MINDSET
AND THE AUTHORS,
GO TO WWW.NEWMONEYMINDSET.COM.

CP1014